THE NEW THINKER'S LIBRARY

General Editor: RAYMOND WILLIAMS

THE UNIVERSITY AS THE NEW CHURCH

THE UNIVERSITY
AS
THE NEW CHURCH

BY
HAZEL E. BARNES

LONDON
C. A. WATTS & CO. LTD.
1970

First published 1970

ISBN 0 296 34841 4

Printed in Great Britain by
Alden & Mowbray Ltd
at the Alden Press, Oxford
36/636

FOR MY FATHER

FOR MY FATHER

PREFACE

THIS book is about the University as it is and as it might be. On occasion I have distinguished between undergraduate colleges and the 'multiversity' as a sprawling complex of liberal arts college, graduate departments, professional schools, and research centres. For the most part, in treating the problems of the University, I have identified them with the question of higher education generally. It was not my intention to limit my discussion to the educational system of any one country, but it will be immediately obvious that my specific examples and proposals reflect the fact that my own teaching experience has been wholly within American institutions. Except for three years at Pierce College, an American school in Greece, I have studied and taught solely in the United States. Consequently, although the book was intended specifically for publication in England, I have written it against the background which is familiar to me in order that I might speak concretely and rely upon first-hand information. I believe that what I have said, if it is valid at all, applies to education everywhere. At times, however, it may be necessary to translate my illustrations and criticisms into their equivalent in Europe or elsewhere – just as any reader will realize that the American 'public school' is a state-supported institution and not comparable to Eton or Harrow.

My criticisms of the University have not sprung from discontent with my individual situation as a professor. I have found my academic career richly rewarding to me personally, and I have only appreciation for the University of Colorado, which has consistently encouraged and supported me in my

teaching and writing. In particular, I take pleasure in acknowledging my indebtedness to the University's Graduate
Council on Research and Creative Work, which granted me
a faculty fellowship for the fall semester in 1969 so that I
might be free to devote all of my time to preparing this
book.

I wish especially to thank Doris J. Schwalbe for reading
and discussing the manuscript with me and for contributing
valuable suggestions.

H. E. B.

Boulder, Colorado
May 1970

CONTENTS

CONTENTS

I

CHURCH AND UNIVERSITY:
PARTNERS IN CRISIS

RADICAL theologians proclaimed the death of God, revolutionary students have temporarily shut down a number of universities. Criticism of the Church and of the University has been carried to the point of questioning whether the existence of either is still justified. These questions have come from within – from clergymen, from students and teachers. The attack has been concentrated on two fronts: each institution has been challenged with respect to the validity, value, and social relevance of what it offers to its members; each has been reproached for inadequately or improperly engaging itself in sociopolitical issues.

It is not surprising that Church and University should be undergoing comparable crises in a period when every one of the human 'givens' has been brought into question – patriotism, the sexual code, the sanctity of marriage and family (including parents' unlimited right to reproduce themselves), private property, distinctions of race and class, the fixed biology of our species, the identity of such terms as 'human' and 'earthly'. When one is forced to recognize that there may be a genuine difference between such formerly interchangeable inquiries as 'Where in the world were you?' and 'Where on earth did you go?' then one realizes that we live our lives as if inside a kaleidoscope which has just been vigorously shaken. Although considerably younger than the family and the tribe, the University and the Church have for so many centuries played major roles in Western civilization that it is all but impossible for most people to conceive of a society without them. Whether or not either is destined to disappear entirely, it seems almost certain that neither will survive for very long without carrying on much further the change in basic patterns which has already started.

The similarity of the situations in which University and Church now find themselves suggests that in their fundamental nature there must be some common likeness. It would be possible, without undue violence, to sum up the goals of each in identical terms: to point out the path to truth, to instruct the young, to guide man toward the good life. When clerics and professors held similar or compatible views on what constitutes truths and Truth and the quality of the good life, then Church and University, if not duplicating each other's functions, differed largely in the emphasis which they placed on serving the Truth through worship or mastering the techniques necessary to live successfully on God's earth. It was a very natural development that in earlier centuries Oxford and Cambridge should be preponderantly training schools for young clergymen or that for two hundred years most American college presidents were ministers. Nor was it surprising that as the University became increasingly secularized, particular religious denominations established new church colleges to ensure that truth and the good life as conceived by the founders should be kept in harmony with the content of the academic curriculum as actually taught.

The two institutions have held somewhat ambiguous relations to the rest of society. Overt claims to temporal power were reluctantly abandoned by the Church by the end of the Renaissance. The University was never in a position to demand governing power outside its own domain, but the continued friction between town and gown was significant of more than the contest between riotous students and the constables. To a certain extent the Church and the University have both been granted, as it were, the privilege of sanctuary. Matters of conscience and freedom to follow to whatever conclusion the pursuit of knowledge might lead were theoretically hereditary rights which the State could not revoke. In return the Church and the University tacitly agreed not to involve themselves in political matters and not to act contrary to society's laws. Independence and neutrality, if not viewed as synonyms, were at least inseparable.

Of course the Church and the University have frequently been at odds with one another – never more so, I suppose, than in the first half of this century when parents were quite right in fearing that some University professors would consider it their duty to rid the student of his naïve philosophical prejudices and provincialism and to open his eyes to a broader and more scientific view of reality. Yet just when it appeared that the separation might be final, a strange paradox came about. As the gap between the two grew wider, each institution began to take on some of the qualities which traditionally had been attached to the other. The Church, to the dismay of many of its members, has tended to become increasingly secular, both in its growing involvement with social and political issues and in its doctrine. Such concepts as the 'death of God' and the 'secular city' were in fact nothing more than the determination to make religion 'this worldly' and to redefine God in such a way that He remains meaningful as a motive force for human love and concern but no longer a serious point of division between Christian and concerned atheist. Rather than continuing to safeguard tradition, the Church has challenged it. Situation ethics and social action are proposed as alternatives for the Ten Commandments and preparation for the next world. The University, too, has been asked to restructure itself and to redefine its purpose in a manner so radical that, as with the Church, compliance would seem to demand that the University abandon or recast what has been its foundation and reason for being. The Church is requested to forsake its preoccupation with eternity and its concern for non-temporal values; the University is told that its dedication to objective truth and scholarship is an evasion of social responsibility and that it ought to give instruction in values. This seems to be almost a reversal of their traditional roles. Another way of putting it would be to say that each is being asked to effect the same transformation – to become an instrument for social change.

It is no wonder that those who would like to return to the day before yesterday see in this common crisis a threat to our whole way of life. In Boulder, Colorado, one such conservative voice is expressed in a series of paid advertisements in the local newspaper. The writer complained forlornly, 'Extremist professors are now substituting revolution for learning in our universities in the same way radical theologians have substituted "humanism" for faith in God'.[1]

Apart from the fact that Church and University face a comparable crisis, I have been interested to note how often, in contemporary commentary, writers find it natural to discuss the problems of the University in terms suggesting that it has already become a sort of Church. Examples range from satire and metaphor to overt analysis of its religious aspects. A glance at a few which I have chosen almost at random may serve as an introduction to my theme and serious proposition: that the University, even before the recent student protests, was rapidly taking over the functions of the Church and that the conflict in which the University is now engaged is a religious war.

The most direct comparison between the Christian Church and the University has been made by Ivan Illich and for

[1] 'Classified Advertising Section' of the *Boulder Daily Camera*, 15 January 1969. The advertiser is E. C. Pickett Loan.

purposes entirely negative. In an address delivered at the first awarding of diplomas at the University of Puerto Rico, Illich claimed that the School is, 'The secular Church of an era which is approaching its end'. Illich comments on its 'folklore'.

The academic procession in which we have just participated evokes the ancient religious procession of clerics and cherubs at Corpus Christi. The Church, one, holy, catholic, and . . . Spanish, has been replaced by another ritual institution: the School, compulsory, untouchable, universal, traditional and . . . North American. Alma Mater holds the place of Santa Mater. Today we attribute to our graduation ceremonies the power of rescuing the poor from the slums as our forefathers attributed to baptism the powers of saving the 'Moor' from Hell. The one great difference between the two Creeds is the following: the observance of the academic rites becomes daily more onerous and more constraining than the observance of the rites of the House of God, even at the worst moments of the Spanish Inquisition. Today the School is confused with education as formerly the Church was confused with religion. The patronage which accrediting agencies confer upon educational institutions in Puerto Rico recalls the patronage of the Kings of Spain toward the Church. Federal aid programmes correspond to the donations of yesterday's kings.[1]

I want to return to the reasons which led Ivan Illich to the conclusion that the school as the *sine qua non* of education is a 'sacred cow'. For the moment we may merely note his

[1] Ivan Illich delivered this speech in Spanish. I have seen it only in a French translation: 'L'École, Cette Vache Sacrée', *Les Temps modernes*, November 1969, pp. 673–83. The points of comparison which the article makes between the Church and the University are startlingly similar to those which I sketched in a lecture given two years earlier. Since my talk was never published and since I was first introduced to Illich's ideas when this article appeared, I feel confirmed in my view that the notion of the University as the new Church is based on more than whimsy.

comparison between the contemporary University and the Church at the height of its power.

John Barth's satiric novel, *Giles Goat-Boy*, links University, Church, and Society in a spectacular travesty of contemporary life. In this fictional world of the future, the University has taken over everything, including the political struggle between East and West, now become the East Campus and West Campus, each with its governing Automatic Computer. The University is a complete, not very efficient, technocracy. It offers the only path to salvation though few are saved (passed), most are damned (flunked). Barth offers a brilliant parody of the Lord's Prayer, addressed to the Grand Tutor, though who he is and whether he any longer even exists remains a question. Possibly he represents both God and our remote University presidents:

> Our Founder, who art omniscient,
> Commencèd be Thy Name.
> Thy college come; Thy Assignments done
> On Campus as beyond the Gate.
> Give us this term Thy termly word.
> And excuse us our cribbing,
> As we excuse classmates who crib from us.
> Lead us not into procrastination,
> But deliver us from error:
> For Thine is the rank, tenure, and seniority, for ever.
> So pass us.[1]

I quote this bit of nonsense because Barth expresses through it a view which many persons take very seriously: that the University now plays a vital role in the socio-political arena, that it is increasingly becoming a way of life for many persons, and that in the process it has become dehumanized, fragmented, and corrupt.

[1] John Barth, *Giles Goat-Boy or, The Revised New Syllabus*, Garden City, Doubleday, 1966, p. 363; London, Secker & Warburg, 1967.

More soberly and with more optimism concerning the possibilities of scientific progress, Desmond Morris (in *The Naked Ape*) extends the traditional faith of the Universities so as to make of it a new religion for our time. As in Barth's novel, Morris sees the Church as having been already replaced by other cultural institutions. He holds that there is a common faith which unites all elements of society:

A belief in the validity of the acquisition of knowledge and a scientific understanding of the world we live in, the creation and appreciation of aesthetic phenomena in all their many forms, and the broadening and deepening of our range of experiences in day-to-day living, is rapidly becoming the 'religion' of our time. Experience and understanding are our rather abstract god-figures, and ignorance and stupidity will make them angry. Our schools and universities are our religious training centres, our libraries, museums, art galleries, theatres, concert halls and sports arenas are our places of communal worship. At home we worship with our books, newspapers, magazines, radios and television sets. In a sense, we still believe in an after-life, because part of the reward obtained from our creative works is the feeling that, through them, we will 'live on' after we are dead. Like all religions, this one has its dangers, but if we have to have one, and it seems that we do, then it certainly appears to be the one most suitable for the unique biological qualities of our species.[1]

Humanism, trust in science and objective truth are the keynotes of this religion. The precepts of the faith are instilled by the schools and universities, 'our religious training centres', but we may note an important point: Desmond Morris is thinking of the educational system as it has been for a long time now, not as it would be restructured by radical students. For him the University is indeed the new Church, but it is the old University.

Morris does not specify what he considers to be the dangers

---

[1] Desmond Morris, *The Naked Ape*, New York, Dell, 1969, pp. 148-9; London, Cape, 1967.

B

of this religion, but many of his contemporaries are eager to point them out. Jencks and Riesman in *The Academic Revolution* discuss this faith as it has been propagated by the universities. If we judge the tree by the fruit, it is proved lacking. Although their long discussion of the growing professionalism in higher education in the United States includes some statements to the effect that teachers know more and students learn more than formerly, the two authors' final summation is a strong indictment. The book is full of metaphors which compare the educational process to the religious quest. In the last chapter, after suggesting certain constructive changes, they write,

Yet these changes, desirable as they are, do not go to the heart of the two central problems of contemporary higher education. The first of these is the academic profession's understandable preference for preaching to the already converted minority instead of doing missionary work among the heathen majority. The second is the inadequacy of the faith most academicians adhere to.[1]

Rebelling students have focused their attacks on both of these problems. They demand that the University open its doors to those previously deemed unworthy of admission. They excoriate not only the quality of much of the teaching they have received but the very ideals of impersonal research and the objective transmission of facts. Going beyond the intent of Jencks and Riesman, some have argued that the University should be closed down temporarily until it can be rebuilt on a different basis. Others would suspend or de-emphasize academic subject-matter in favour of the discussion of world politics and projects for social reform. All plead that the classroom should be made more relevant though they do not always specify exactly what they mean by the term,

[1] Christopher Jencks and David Riesman, *The Academic Revolution*, Garden City, Doubleday, 1968, p. 513.

nor is it probable that we would find complete agreement if they were all to define it precisely.

Everywhere in the student protests one may be aware of an aura of the religious. I do not mean simply that there is the fervour of intense commitment to a cause – whether it be Maoism or Black militancy or social revolution. Nor do I refer solely to the fact that those involved in the movement are known to be frequently concerned with investigating the possibilities of Eastern religion, cosmic consciousness, and the like. There have been more serious implications.

Philip Toynbee in 1968 declared that the student revolt was 'more like a religious than a political or economic movement'. He listed, in support of his statement, eight things which he found to be characteristic of most of the student activists:

(1) the return to absolute values, (2) the desire for personal purity, (3) hatred of 'the world', (4) a metaphysical use of the word 'real' (as in 'real presence') by which an apparent reality is contrasted with a 'more real' reality which can be perceived only by the initiates, (5) thus the inevitable élitism of 'the saved', (6) combined with a firm rejection of empiricism amounting at times to a rejection of history, (7) the existence of holy writ (Marcuse, Fanon, Guevara, Mao, Debray, Reich), (8) the worship of a god or gods in human form.[1]

Toynbee admits that this summation contains some exaggeration and that it does not apply to all student leaders. I myself would object to at least one of his points. It seems to me that, far from rejecting empiricism and history, student leaders are acutely aware that they are making history and are particularly eager not to repeat the mistakes of older generations. This attitude is responsible for the reluctance of most to organize themselves into political parties and their

[1] Philip Toynbee, 'Intolerable', *The Observer Review*, 23 June 1968, pp. 21-2.

preference to remain 'issue oriented'. Against the cynicism of their elders they assert that old patterns need not be repeated and that something entirely different may be brought into being. This faith in the possibility of a new world and a cleansed society strikes me as perhaps the most unmistakably religious aspect of the movement. Yet fundamentally Toynbee is right. The student upheaval cannot be reduced to simply one more chapter in the perennial revolt of the young against established authority nor to a series of local struggles to abolish irksome regulations of campus life. It goes beyond the University in its implications, and it seeks openly to provide a changed way of living for everyone.

Many persons who recognize that there is a religious quality in the reproaches levelled against the University object for exactly this reason: that it is inappropriate to confuse the intellectual sphere with the spiritual. An example is Thomas A. Langford, who might be said to combine already in his own person the union of church and university inasmuch as he is himself the Chairman of the Department of Religion at the University of North Carolina. Professor Langford writes sympathetically of the students, he feels that at least some of their demands are religious in nature, expressing genuine and vital needs which are not being satisfied anywhere in contemporary society. In an article called 'Campus Turmoil: A Religious Dimension',[1] he is concerned with only one of the student appeals, but it is one which – especially in the United States – has been voiced frequently and urgently. This is the insistence that the University has become too impersonal and that it ought to remake itself so that it would offer to the student the opportunity of entering into a true 'community of persons' which would include professors as well as other students. Langford

[1] Thomas A. Langford, 'Campus Turmoil: A Religious Dimension', *The Christian Century*, 8 February 1967, pp. 172-4.

feels that the student seeks this meaningful interpersonal relation within the University as a last hope because he has failed to find it in the family or church or earlier in the educational system. He argues, however, that no matter how legitimate the need, it is one which the present multiversity is incapable of satisfying because of its sheer complexity and the pressure of manifold commitments on the part of the faculty. One might expect that at this point Langford would discuss possibilities of correcting the situation at the University, but that is far from his intention. He emphasizes that the student's failure to find significant human relations at the University parallels his earlier failure to discover through the Church a genuine relation with God. But he has no plan and apparently no desire to hunt for ways by which the University might succeed in the human sphere. For Langford, the spiritual value for which the young are searching cannot be found in interpersonal relations. 'The ultimately valid relationship is the relationship of man with God.' To perceive this truth is to lift from human relationships a burden which they are incapable of supporting. Langford concludes that the University cannot successfully take over the functions of the Church any more than human relations can 'carry the totality of spiritual meaning'. Although the witness of Christian faith should 'translate faithful life with God into life on the campus', clearly, on Langford's view, the University is not to tamper with spiritual matters and presumably not with the world of values. His solution for this problem in the University, at least so far as this article is concerned, is simply to hand it back to the Church. How that institution will cope with it in the future when, by Langford's own admission, it has failed up to now, is not made clear. Nor does he suggest any method for persuading the students that they are addressing themselves to the administration of the wrong institution.

Many persons who would not share Professor Langford's confidence in the power of a reawakened Church will nevertheless agree most emphatically that questions of morality, social justice, and values for living do not belong within the province of the University. I have often wondered where they do fall if not in the hands of the educators. Some answers come from the public media, to be sure, but this source is neither systematic, complete, nor wholly reliable. Moreover it presupposes that one has developed the capacity to judge between its many contradictions, its facts and falsities, realities and distortions. Should instruction as to how to live in this world come solely from the family and particularly from the parents? If ever there was a time when basic human attitudes were transmitted in unbroken tradition from one generation to the next, independent of historical changes, this time is beyond the memory of most of us. Parents are but grown-up children who at best take the time to share with their offspring the attitudes which they themselves have learned from experience. I suspect that in the minds of most of the people who argue that teachers ought to teach facts and not values, there is the vague belief that a person should pick his own morality and social attitudes in the same way that he selects the person he wants to marry, and that psychiatrists, like marriage counsellors, exist to help those who fall into difficulty. Yet while I cannot commend too strongly the idea that each individual should be free to work out the particular code and system of values to which he can honestly commit himself, I believe that for almost everybody such learning is accomplished more effectively where there has been appropriate teaching than where there has not. It is my conviction that a significant degree of crime, violence, and shattered lives is due precisely to the fact that the majority of people have seldom if ever been in a situation where for a sustained period they were forced to examine carefully

the values by which they will continue unthinkingly to
live.

For the most part in contemporary culture there is no
built-in plan whereby no person may come of age without
having been exposed to thoughtful discussions of personal
value systems and social responsibilities. (I exclude those
required courses in political indoctrination of the young
which exist in some Communist countries. We may observe,
however, that their establishment is due to the realization by
political leaders that one cannot expect people to develop
desired social attitudes unless some sort of training is given.)
If we were to grant that some definite programme is desirable, I can think of only three likely candidates to whom we
might entrust the main burden of responsibility. These are
psychological counsellors, the church, and the schools.

For many individuals the psychiatrist has long since
replaced the parish priest, receiving the same confessions,
offering different but comparable forms of penance and
absolutions. The gifted psychotherapist may well lead his
patient to a psychic rebirth as significant and at least as
enduring as the old-fashioned religious conversion. A school
child or adolescent with delinquent tendencies or obviously
disturbed patterns of human relations will be aided, if he
receives any help at all, by the staff psychologist. I do not
discount the importance of these contributions, but neither
do I propose that in the future we should entrust to psychologists the task of taking care of man's spiritual and ethical
needs. The idea is perhaps not quite so bizarre as it appears
at first glance. Granted that today those who work in the
field of mental health think of themselves as healers of the
ill, there is no compelling reason why their efforts should be
limited to repair work. One can at least imagine a society
in which at a certain period of his life everyone would receive
some rudimentary instruction in psychological principles

which would help him to understand himself and others. Who more natural than the psychotherapist to equip us for dealing with problems of self-fulfilment and those social evils which obstruct personal development? Yet somehow I cannot see the psychiatrist's couch transformed successfully into a pulpit, nor do I think that it is in psychology by itself that we will find the answer to what the students demand. Those who practise it claim that psychology is a science. Personally I believe it is both more and less than that. It would be straining to the breaking point if we demanded that these theorists of the psyche should become teachers of the human soul and doctors of the world.

Why not, then, simply leave the whole matter of values and social conscience with the Church, particularly since its contemporary leaders have shown that they are prepared to go beyond its outmoded theology and have demonstrated their willingness to make social commitments and to undertake social actions? There are several objections. First, if we are to assume that we are talking about existing churches, they cannot serve everybody. A church (i.e. the organized community of any church or synagogue or temple) is committed to some kind of metaphysical hypothesis and has been established to satisfy the desire of certain individuals to worship or feel themselves in communion with something more than the everyday world. Even if its theology has become so 'demythologized' as to be little more than a resolve to make of the teachings of Jesus or Buddha or the Old Testament prophets an ideal for living, still the central motivation is one which many other persons cannot accept. I do not object to diversity as such. A variety of approaches to the discussion of values is the only insurance against totalitarian indoctrination and repression. But I am against the idea that there is a necessary connection between either the felt need for community worship or metaphysical hypotheses and the necessity of confronting and taking appropriate action with respect to moral and social issues in the contemporary world. Furthermore, I do not believe that even in the most radical of religious institutions we can find anything remotely resembling the kind of total instruction in ethical understanding which as a society we desperately need.

The great affirmation of the Western Church in our century is its rediscovery of Love. This has transformed both the sermons and the weekday activities of individual clergymen and in some instances the life of their congregations. Priests and pastors, often without the approval of the majority of their flock, have taken the lead in civil rights and anti-war demonstrations. God as the supporting source of all human love, and love as the criterion for all ethical conduct – the two notions combined have stimulated church leaders to involve themselves more directly and forcefully in social action than anything the world has witnessed for generations. They have continued to act by the stern resolve to take whatever steps are necessary to wipe out obvious examples of injustice and oppression whether local or global. The Church has rediscovered heroism and even martyrdom. Less spectacular but perhaps more revolutionary has been the change in its teaching of personal ethics – the new morality.

This is not the place to discuss the philosophical validity of situation ethics, but one or two remarks seem relevant and necessary. First, one can hardly over-emphasize the degree to which the new morality constitutes a breakthrough in the impasse in which the modern church had found itself. So long as morality was thought of as a set of positive and negative prescriptions, clerical authorities had to choose between holding on to an archaic code totally out of harmony with the ever-changing life of man or else face the continuing task of adjusting its regulations, with inevitable inconsistencies and with no hope of satisfying everyone that the new interpretations were the correct ones. In situation ethics there are no rules. Every moral decision must be made within the context of its own situation, and all situations are unique. The touchstone value is love. As Joseph Fletcher summarizes, 'Love only is always good. Love is the only norm. Love and justice are the same'. Fletcher properly distinguishes love from simple personal liking and from mindless sentimentality. With hardheaded realism he argues that of course the end must justify the means since nothing else can, but he points out that every end, too, is relative and can be justified as such only if it serves the cause of love.

To the extent to which this kind of thinking can open the minds of people so that they are willing to reconsider those absolute rules which institutionally and in the law courts have restricted everything from sexual relations and observance of the Sabbath to the length of school children's hair and skirts, it comes to us like a stream of pure oxygen in the midst of the smog. But like that pure gas, it carries its own dangers and can produce destructive explosions if one is not careful. Mr. Fletcher's own discussion of an example illustrates in part why I feel that we cannot entrust the problem of values even to the new, sophisticated, and socially conscious church. Fletcher reports his conversation with a woman who had been asked by a national intelligence agency if she would deliberately involve herself in a sexual affair so as to set up a trap to blackmail an enemy spy. Apparently both saw the problem as a dilemma posed by the two conflicting demands of safeguarding a personal sexual code and duty to one's country. 'We discussed it as a question of patriotic prostitution and personal integrity . . . how was she to balance loyalty and gratitude as an American citizen over against her ideal of sexual integrity?'[1] I myself was appalled

[1] Joseph Fletcher, *Situation Ethics*, Philadelphia, Westminster Press, 1966, pp. 163-4; London, S.C.M. Press, 1966.

to read this statement. To me far more is involved than sexual purity versus patriotism, both of which are taken as evident goods. Is the violation of human trust for the sake of blackmail any less questionable than infringement of a personal sexual code? Is this kind of procedure a legitimate enterprise on the part of our State Department? If one participates in it, is one being patriotic or working to impair still further an immoral government? Finally, were the national aims which were to be furthered by all this counter-espionage of a kind that a thoughtful citizen could approve or not? Possibly Mr. Fletcher thought of these issues. I am sure in any case that the differences in our appraisals of the situation would only strengthen his argument that all ethical decisions are relative to the one who makes them. But the example points up the obvious though trite idea that love is not enough. Even if we reduce this particular decision to a choice of self-love as compared with love of one's country, there must be hidden within the process of decision some crude sort of hedonistic calculus. Furthermore, even in this private problem, we are referred to a host of considerations where knowledge and the thoughtful appraisal of the background issues are essential. They cannot be accomplished in the relatively small period when the critical decision must be made. A defensible decision within the context of situation ethics demands a long period of study of the social context as well as self-awareness of the techniques of self-deception within us. The Church can do much as a leader of action in those few areas where the issue is clear, where the obvious evil to be corrected is glaring, and where the primary goal is to influence the general public and to force authorities to apply or to formulate just legislation. It can provide fellowship for men and women whose metaphysical hypotheses are similar, and it can provide a ritual or formal worship for those who still find it meaningful. I do not believe that it can possibly serve as a training ground to develop within either child or adult the complex of personal and social values which will manifest itself in active involvement in building a better world and which demands the critical use of specific knowledge. In short, I am convinced that the Church is incapable of satisfying the student demands for a reappraisal of values and the restructuring of society and that this would be true even if we were able and willing to persuade everyone to attend the church of his choice.

This leaves us with the University. More accurately I should say that it is the educational institutions taken all together which offer a third possibility for the planned teaching of values. It is possible that changes in elementary and secondary schools may ultimately prove to be the most critical in influencing the human character. Certainly it would make no sense to leave the lower schools untouched while drastically revising the whole intellectual enterprise at the college and university level. But it is the existence of the University and the nature of its undergraduate and graduate admission requirements which primarily determine the quality of education from the first grade on – not to mention the fact that the University trains future teachers. Among those who clamour for abolition, reorganization, or reform of the University and those who think that requests for restructuring and redefining educational goals and methods amount to a plea for destroying what we now know as the University, there is usually one common, tacit assumption. This is the belief that the University as it has been for the last fifty years has in fact devoted itself exclusively to the training of students by impartially imparting facts, that the University, like the Church, is concerned with one sphere of human activity only – in this case the intellectual – and that it remains detached, apart from politics and from the rest of society. It is my conviction that the view of the University as the manufacturer of living encyclopedias is not only wrong and out-dated but downright false. I do not claim that the revolt of the students is without cause. What I mean rather is this – that over the last half century the University, particularly in America, has been in truth becoming a Church to the point of duplicating our religious institutions in function if not rendering them obsolete. Under the guise of detachment and non-commitment, the University has been handling the problems of values surreptitiously and performing its religious duties badly. It has become a Church without ever clearly formulating its faith or seriously examining the worth of its plan for salvation. I believe that whatever we may think of what student protesters propose for the future, they are right in thinking that in the University rests the best, perhaps the only, hope of initiating significant changes in the life of man.

The thought that the University had gradually slipped into the role and assumed many of the functions of the traditional Western Church occurred to me some time before the student unrest began to reveal itself as an incipient revolution. At that time, I confess, it came to me mostly as an idea to play with; I derived a mild enjoyment from parallels which struck me as more amusing than significant. Naturally the compari-son did not hold exactly. Of the three ancient vows of chastity, obedience, and poverty, only the last remained and this largely as a transitional stage for graduate students and beginning instructors. On the other hand we may note that when Heavenly Visitors were reported as coming to earth in extra-terrestrial chariots, it was a University physicist and not a Bishop who was put in charge of investigating the reality of the unidentified flying objects. And it did seem to me that much of professorial activity was devoted to keeping alive the achievements of past cultures which the outside world would just as soon forget in its concentration on present and future. Like the medieval Church, the University appeared to have appointed itself as guardian of the talents. As in the New Testament story, some were using their inheritance to achieve new riches while others jealously guarded what came to them, allowing it neither to disappear nor to grow. We have had our equivalents to those monks who devoted themselves to illuminating the margins of manuscripts or adding commentaries to earlier works, spending their lives in servitude to 'the apparatus of scholarship which serves so many men as a substitute for thought'.[1] In a different way, the early student love-ins and be-ins suggested the love feasts of old-style evangelical churches. The University has gradually come to dominate much of community life in a manner which bears a certain resemblance to the combination of spiritual authority and temporal power held by the medieval Church, and this parallel has certain disturbing aspects. It has become increasingly obvious that without the offices of University and College, without the degree which serves as a baptismal certificate, few can be saved economically or socially. The thought of what the future holds in store for the bright young heretic who has been excommunicated is appalling. And speaking of heresy, we observe that today's Temple of Reason must fight to preserve the purity of its dogma. The ancient heretical tendency to pantheism has reappeared. Seemingly true believers are led astray by the false doctrines of Huxley and Isherwood or de Chardin. Perhaps the psychedelics are our Anabaptists.

More seriously, it is evident that the University is fast becoming the centre of community cultural life. It keeps distinguished writers and artists on its payroll. For the general public, it provides drama, concerts, lectures, artistic productions of all kinds, created either by its own members or by those travelling groups or individuals who are paid to come

[1] This description is taken from Jencks and Riesman, op. cit., pp. 299-300.

and perform. As the root meanings of the words suggest, the *catholic* church and the *university* have, each in its turn, undertaken to minister to the whole of society and to unify all aspects of human activity. Education, even when it restricts itself to the imparting of information, has long since ceased to be concerned solely with the training of the young. Some graduate students have to be discouraged from making it a permanent way of life. There are evening courses for adults who want to study for 'non-credit', correspondence courses for persons who want to work toward a degree but cannot attend classes on campus. Even those courses formally designed for young people preparing for a career are generously sprinkled with older persons who return to college or attend for the first time – married women whose children are now off to school, men who want to change their type of employment or to advance farther within their professions, retired people, or those with leisure who want to study for the sheer pleasure of learning or as an alternative to boredom.

The University is often reproached for not meeting its social obligations. There may be some justification for the attack. At the same time it has for a long time now been deeply involved in those social enterprises which some centuries ago were part of the works of charity offered by the Church. Hospitals sometimes, of course, still maintain a link with a religious denomination. They are often and more significantly related to a university medical school. A few churches still hold bazaars to collect money for the poor and send their missionaries abroad. The idealism of college students in recent years has been leading them more frequently to the Peace Corps and Vista. On the domestic front it is social engineering which on a day-to-day basis has replaced the kindly activity of the working priests and good women of the parish. Whether or not these varied projects for social improvement are actually initiated and run by the University (and often they are), it is the sociologists, social workers, and psychologists who implement them, having been scientifically trained in their respective academic departments. Economic planning, too, often derives directly from University research or is worked out by professors summoned by the Government and on leave from their University positions. Constantly the University is denounced for its alliance with the military-industrial complex. We can only hope that the competition for research grants carries with it no taint of simony. The University has its own representatives at Court in the various committees and lobbies which it maintains at Washington. The President of the United States frequently chooses members of his Cabinet from University faculty, much as the Kings of England and France sought counsel and were threatened by the powerful cardinals. The question of the non-taxation of University property has recently become an issue in this country, reminding us of the ancient accusation against the Church – that it enriched itself with its vast holdings of lucrative, untaxable land.

There is another area in which both Church and University have shown interest; this is eschatology, formally defined as the 'doctrine of last things' but referring more generally to all serious consideration or speculation about the future destination of man and the course of human history. It is interesting to observe that here the Church has all but given up its active concern whereas the University has usurped the field more and more. For centuries preparation for the Last Judgment and Eternal Life was the Church's reason for being. The ultimate destruction of the world was anticipated as an inevitable historical development; clergymen argued about such details as whether a millennium of peace on earth would precede or follow the second coming of Christ. Personal immortality was so assured that one, so to speak, purchased tickets of admission by consenting to receive the sacraments. Today still there are some people who cherish the literal hope of the eternal survival of their very personal selves; there are many pulpits where the phrase 'eternal life' is commonplace. For the most part the word 'immortality' is used almost metaphorically, pointing to a mystery, indicating an undefined hope that in some way beyond our comprehension we will participate in the ongoing life of the universe. To be sure, the proclamation that 'God is dead' has been reinterpreted by most churchmen to mean that our relationship with him has come to a dead end and that we must search for new ways in which to experience him. Some feel that God has withdrawn and left to us humans the task of taking care of the world and determining the direction of history. Very few would care to attribute the horrors of recent years to any express intention on the part of the Deity. We are bidden to hope for God's return at a time when we are better prepared to entertain him. A few theologians still claim to tune into God for encouragement. The average theologian would be highly embarrassed to confess that he expected to survive as his individual self. The Bishop Pikes who argue that the worlds of living and dead have a private communication service are rare indeed.

In contrast the University embraces openly a prophetic view of the future. But with a decisive difference. The Church has based its eschatology on past revelation and the faith that what has been revealed and promised will be accomplished. It has become less prophetic as it has grown less fundamentalist and less literal in its use of sacred writing. Within the University and in society generally we are increasingly aware of ourselves as creators, not revealers of a new kind of future for mankind, as authors of the historical process, not as actors bound by fidelity to a preconceived text. This consciousness of moulding the ongoing life of man and

C

the world in our very attempts to study and understand it is most obvious in the scientists, who realize more fully than their predecessors that the experimenter stands inside the experimental field and not outside in some neutral territory. This fact is equally true for all seekers after knowledge. Already the law has been forced to take cognizance of some of the implications of recent breakthroughs in medicine, notably in the area of organ transplants with the possibility of extended longevity for the lucky few. Astrogeophysics and research for space projects open the door to human adventures which could conceivably destroy us as a species or change our lives qualitatively in ways presently beyond our imagination. Von Braun did not exaggerate when he made the statement, 'What we will have attained when Neil Armstrong steps down upon the moon is a completely new step in the evolution of man'.[1] Biologists, in their developments in genetic coding, now recognize that man is in a position to direct his further development as a species. Less spectacular but perhaps more immediately relevant to us and just as future-oriented is the work of the social scientists. As a single example, I may mention the new concept of action research, study projects in which the experimenters strive to introduce constructive changes into the social milieu which they are investigating. Nor let anyone be so naïve as to think, despite the scholar's traditional long established commitment to the ideal of objectivity, that the judgments of historians are wholly without relevance to present or future or that political science and economics are purely descriptive. Objectivity may frequently pass as a covert defence of the *status quo*, but today's social scientist is much too sophisticated to believe any longer that facts as presented are uninfluenced by the one who reports them. As for the humanities, we need only think of

1 Quoted by Norman Mailer, 'A Fire on the Moon', *Life*, 29 August 1969, p. 34.

McLuhan, who has already proclaimed the end of the Gutenberg era and heralded the arrival of the global village. Linguists, psychologists, writers and other artists – all those who have suddenly become aware of the extent to which man's language and senses have structured the nature of what he has held to be objective experience – demonstrate to us that, as we think and perceive, so are we and that neither the forms of language nor of thought are fixed. We might say that in today's University, as in the medieval Church, there are some thinkers who seek to inspire us by helping us to rediscover the rich treasures of past revelation and others who urge us to consider our actions as steps toward another kind of existence. For the Church, the danger lay in too narrowly defining this future in the light of an earlier vision. For the University the peril lies in the possibility of our becoming so absorbed in the process itself that we fail to ask ourselves what, if any, kind of ideal is directing this movement forward. If eschatological theologians sometimes seemed to believe that we might move forward confidently by the gleam of a candle fixed behind us, today's scientific guides toward the future tend to move relentlessly onward without stopping to take counsel as to the best direction or to consider the possible effects of the new territory on the health of us travellers.

Some of the problems and accusations which the University has been forced to face are curiously akin to those which the Church confronted at the height of its power. Perhaps the most obvious is the age-old question of reason versus revelation. Both the validity of ecclesiastical doctrine and the authority of the hierocracy were challenged again and again by individuals claiming to have received divine communication inspiring them with new truth or deeper insight into the meaning of earlier sacred proclamation. The Church was firmly established on the principle that both reason and revelation are necessary but that revelation takes precedence chronologically and logically. Man's awareness of divine Presence is a continuing event in history. Hence the Church could not deny the occurrence of new revelation any more than it could reject miracles, and it was forced to distinguish officially between saint and heretic. In this way it allowed scope for its own gradual evolution while protecting itself against total upheaval. The parallel with the University is laughably close. Academic history offers an assortment of heretics later made into saints – Schliemann, Schopenhauer, Nietzsche, Darwin. Today bears witness to the same capriciousness as to what does or does not constitute heresy. Timothy Leary lost his job at Harvard; students who experiment with LSD are expelled or arrested or both. Professors who carry on research in the use of hallucinogenic drugs receive federal grants. Departments of philosophy appoint professors to teach oriental philosophy and expect these classes to be guided by the trust in the superiority of rationality which has been the hallmark of Western thinkers. Meanwhile Marshall McLuhan is a highly paid cardinal at the university of Toronto and well on the road to canonization. In my opinion McLuhanism offers a far more serious threat to orthodox academicism than Timothy Leary's neo-primitivism. Of course the Church was able to shelter both Aquinas and St Francis; perhaps the University, too, is learning.

At present the University is being challenged to assume openly the role of guardian of conscience. Those who regard the demand as inappropriate should realize that it springs from seeds which the University itself has planted. Its tradition of pursuing truth at all cost has not always led to a policy of welcoming revolutionary and uncomfortable truths. Yet the University has generally held to the view that at least the other side should be heard. Classroom discussions of social theories and of the moral dilemmas of literary heroes and heroines were forerunners of the teach-ins on Vietnam and civil rights. It was unusual but not unnatural that, when Martin Luther King was assassinated in 1968, many classes were suspended for a day so that professors and students might participate in seminars and discussion groups to explore the nature and pass judgment on the morality of our national policies. Questions of ethical responsibility have not been strangers in classes in humanities and the social sciences though they have been restricted, for the most part, to abstract theoretical discussion. It is significant that part of the impetus for the student revolt stems from the easily perceived discrepancy between what the professors preached and what the University and the rest of society practised. Religious and academic hypocrisy have much in common.

Along with the reproach that they have been socially irrelevant, the Church and the University have been charged with another sin, and I think that both must plead guilty. Each has to some degree demanded that its members look on their present existence as preparation for the 'real life' to come. The Church has had to face up to the charge of other-worldliness for some time now. The University has attempted to prolong the adolescence of students, in effect asking them to study now and live later. In both cases restrictions have been placed on free thought and action, the present being sacrificed to the future. With these thoughts in mind, one may be inclined to take a different view of actions which some older people have wanted to dismiss as irresponsible lack of discipline and rowdiness. When students at the university of Colorado, in a peaceful demonstration, presented the request that they be allowed unrestricted hetero-sexual visiting in each other's rooms, this act was partly to protest the University's right of being *in loco parentis* and to demand that as adults they should be allowed to solve their

own personal problems. Even more significantly it represented their desire to persuade the University Administration
to commit itself in support of a new code of sexual morality
and thereby to take the lead in forcing the rest of society to
acknowledge that a change in values had come about. Properly
interpreted, the event was not a manifestation of undisci-
plined adolescent rebellion against reasonable authority but
rather a serious declaration that the students had come of age
and that the University should take a stand on a moral issue.

One could continue indefinitely the search for parallels
between the University and the Church. One may find
suggestions of a split between intellectuals and non-intellectuals which at least suggests the division between clergy and
laity, perhaps also an incipient conflict between the Church-
University and State. One might ask whether the student
revolt is a simple heresy or a new Protestant secession to be
followed by a Council of Trent and a Counter-Reformation.
But further extension would quickly become merely whim-
sical or misleading. The point which I have tried to make is
that the University has already progressed far beyond the
point where it can truthfully claim to be concerned only with
the neutral transmission of knowledge. It has always been
committed to a definite set of values whether acknowledged
or undefined. It is inextricably involved with social change,
the moulding of the future. Education today is as neutral
as a virus. What the protesting students demand is not so
much that the University should *become* a religious institution
as that it should change its religion.

Whatever one may think about the Deity's state of health,
the Church of the past is fast becoming a mausoleum. Some
of these rich tombs of the Great retain a certain nostalgic
splendour and are well worth a contemplative visit now and
then. The tourists who come to admire the architecture of
the cathedral of Notre Dame far outnumber those who

worship there. With the exception of a few fundamentalists, the persons to whom Christianity or Judaism means most are those who insist that it be reborn.

It is fashionable these days to seek a comparison between the Western World of our own age and that of the late Roman Empire. Usually the analogy is drawn in a spirit of disillusion and sad resignation. The speaker points to the imperialism of our leading powers, the affluence of the ruling classes alongside the poverty of the oppressed, the decline of moral values and religious faith, the probable coming of a new age of darkness to be brought on by the inner decay of our civilization and the attack of a new tribe of barbarians from without. For my part, I do not foresee a successor to Mao or Kenyatta swooping down upon us like Attila the Hun. (I waive the question of the correctness of thinking of either as a barbarian.) I do not believe that either the violence in the streets or the corruption and repression of government or racial conflict or our systematic destruction of the natural environment is comparable to an irreversible chemical reaction which once started must go on to the inevitable explosion. One may find patterns in history, but they are never repeated exactly; it is doubtful if the people living in a given era could ever be sure as to just what pattern they were in. I will admit to a feeling of there being a different kind of resemblance between the twentieth century and the last centuries of the Roman Empire though I think that it is due to our own historical interpretation of what was happening then rather to a genuine likeness between our reactions and the people of that period. What seems to me most valid in this comparison is the sense of moving from one dispensation to another, an impression which I am sure we experience partly because the existence of past historical patterns helps to shape our own self-consciousness. It is the mood expressed in T. S. Eliot's 'Journey of the Magi'.

Were we led all that way for
Birth or Death? There was a Birth, certainly,
We had evidence and no doubt. I had seen birth and death,
But had thought they were different; this Birth was
Hard and bitter agony for us, like Death, our death.
We returned to our places, these Kingdoms,
But no longer at ease here, in the old dispensation,
With an alien people clutching their gods.[1]

This feeling that we are somehow already separated from past generations and that we do not as yet know or understand the new world whose borders we have just crossed is perhaps the one thing which links the two sides of the generation gap. It is to be expected that youth would look forward eagerly to clearing a dwelling place in the new territory while their elders think nostalgically of the dearly familiar things left behind. But that we have already crossed over, only the self-blinded would deny, and it is not necessarily a good thing to stick as closely as possible to the boundary line in the hope that here the terrain will not have changed too much.

In Italy in the fourth century, literal belief in the ancestral deities was found, if at all, among the uneducated, especially in the remote countryside. A scholarly Roman seeking to interpret his period and the imminent future might have wondered whether Christianity or one of the other popular cults of Eastern mysticism would win out, replacing the old gods completely. He might just as well have believed that the new allegorical and philosophical demythologizing of the Olympian pantheon, as presented by Sallustius, for example, offered an intellectually respectable way of clinging to the traditional religious forms of his ancestors. He could have

---

[1] T. S. Eliot, 'Journey of the Magi', *Collected Poems 1909-1935*, New York, Harcourt Brace & Company, 1936, pp. 125-6; London, Faber & Faber, 1936.

been convinced that the ultimate answer had been provided a century or so earlier by that Tillich-like Neoplatonist Plotinus, who offered to his contemporaries a belief in a God beyond God, a transcendent deity who was also imminent, the Ground of our Being, who or which cannot be denied because He/It is what we are in the depths of our Being. Or our Roman might, like the late Stoics, have been uninterested in pedantic, unprofitable speculation about metaphysical details but actively dedicated to fostering the ideal of the brotherhood of mankind in a Universe where all are manifestations of one Reality.

I do not wish to press for further parallels but rather to stress two things in our imaginary encounter across the ages. The first is the obvious but important fact that the triumph of Christianity, for better or for worse, was only the result of the fact that individuals chose, one after the other, to commit themselves to it. There was no metaphysical action by Historical Necessity. One may find reasons now to explain this choice and the actions consequent on it, but this is to speak after the event, to trace the formation of patterns which did come about but might not have been. Second, I wish quite arbitrarily to present my own reaction to this parallel so far as the contemporary Church is concerned and the University, too. In my opinion contemporary theologians who cling to the name of Christianity, while radically transforming everything which it meant to its founders and to those who until quite recently believed that they and the first followers of Christ worshipped the same God, are attempting a task as futile as that of the belated re-interpreters of the Graeco-Roman pantheon. Also, I do not believe that there will be further divine revelation or that a Messiah will come whose followers can sweep us onward into a new dispensation of belief in a religious order with its own promise of salvation and rebirth for civilization.

What is the probable future of the Western Church which can neither stand still nor retreat to its former position? The most conservative elements would like to delimit its functions more drastically than ever before. This is, of course, one way to safeguard it, but it is also to draw its fangs, to halt its growth, to guarantee a slow death as a dreary alternative to radical transformation. Many such voices have been heard from congregations, arguing that the function of the Church is to give comfort and sustenance to its members rather than to engage in political and social battles. It should, in short, provide communion on Sunday and ignore the weekdays' toil. It is conceivable that the Church might endure a little longer in this way, making concessions to more modern ritual, never raising distressing questions of the relation between its contemporary theology and the historical foundation of its sacred doctrine. I cannot conceive that such a Church will appeal to very many or for long. It is significant that the only successful ecumenical movement has involved progressive churches and not conservative ones. What has united them, however, in so far as it has been something more than a last ditch stand against atheism, has been the resolution to make Christianity more relevant to the contemporary world.

If we look at the truly radical churches and churchmen, we find two tendencies. The first is to subordinate all other considerations to social service – to take the Church out into the street. Certainly on a short term basis, there are congregations which are accomplishing something of real significance in this respect. The concrete existence of the church or synagogue provides a focal point for a kind of community action which could not exist without it. So long as the members of a group share a common philosophical view which recognizes loving concern for one's fellow man as an imperative, they may work effectively to stimulate and support one another in constantly questioning the justice of social realities and in correcting them. Yet, as the nature of the metaphysical commitment is increasingly weakened and departicularized, I see nothing to guarantee the existence of these groups beyond the life of their present constituents. Nor do I see any advantage or durability in them as compared with secular groups of concerned citizens in specific communities, whether politically organized or not. A second tendency is to replace both theology and social ethics with the exploration of consciousness – either by mind-expanding drugs or by new kinds of psychological awareness (e.g. the sensitivity group). One outcome of this is the establishment of small communes where like-minded people may enjoy close fellowship in a community based on respect for a particular set of values chosen and shared by all. On the whole, I am in favour of the existence of such enclaves for those who want to assert their separation from the majority, and I would favour their encouragement in any society, however utopian. But I think that, like the movement toward social service, this new emphasis serves not only to get the congregation out of the church building but to keep it permanently outside the Church as an institution.

It is not my purpose either to predict or to help hasten the early demise of the Church as we have known it. What I wish to argue is rather that its future seems to lie in the direction of satisfying the partial needs of special and diverse groups. I cannot see any indication anywhere that it can do for the whole of society, or even for a particular nation, what the Catholic Church did for Europe or Judaism for the ancient Israelites; that is, provide a world outlook in which man's metaphysical hypotheses, psychological needs, knowledge of the universe, ethical code, and social structure are combined in one great synthesis. I hasten to add that I sincerely hope that never again in the world's history will man be cursed with so strict a dogmatism and forced unanimity of belief as have from time to time been associated with both Christianity and Judaism. I am not arguing for any closed system of indoctrination which might once again be justified by the belief that it represents an ultimate and unsurpassable view of truth. Some degree of libertarianism and pluralism seems to me essential if the individual as such is to retain his unique value.

Yet the old paradox remains true: that only with the help of others can the child learn to be and to think for himself, that each man can be free only if he lives in a state whose laws protect him from institutionalized oppression as well as from the arbitrary violence of other free persons. I wish that there might be guaranteed for ever for everyone access to a wide area where he can work out and live by his own personally created system of values. The existence of this open breathing space, as it were, depends on a common view of man and society which allows and supports it, just as surely as the biological existence of future individuals depends upon present decisions relative to the biological evolution of our species and population control. Ethical decisions, personal and social, cannot be made intelligently without knowledge of facts and a comprehension of reality, by which I suppose we mean understanding this earth and the universe in which it moves as well as human reality. Present and coming generations need to be taught the facts of existence; they need instruction, guidance, and *practice* in making evaluative appraisals. There should be some institution which can serve these needs, which can both guide society and be guided by its members, which can influence political action without being subject to the vagaries of party politics. To some degree the University is and does this, but it does it badly because it has been unwilling to acknowledge that its role involves something more than impartially teaching the facts and techniques which the young must master in order to live in the real world of adults later on.

Where should a young person turn today if he seriously wishes to understand himself, his true relation to his fellow citizens and to his state, his position relative to the past and probable future history of the human race, the nature of the universe? He cannot expect to find adequate answers in either the traditional Church or one of its radicalized off-shoots. For some persons the Church may add a perfecting personal touch, it may serve to channel energies and resolutions made on the basis of information and knowledge gleaned elsewhere. If one wants knowledge of self and others, of history, and of the nature of the universe, one must turn to psychology, to sociology, to all of the sciences and social sciences and humanities – in short to the world of the intellect. I should like to say that he will find his answers in the University, but the army of student protesters has risen up to declare that this is not the case. Nevertheless I think that it ought to be. I seriously propose that the University should become the new church. It is my conviction that it has long been functioning as a church, by which I mean that it has defined truth and human good and taught values as well as knowledge for many years but surreptitiously and without admitting the fact. I think it high time for us to admit that it is wholly wrong, if it is even possible, to discuss the history and present state of human endeavours as if in a moral vacuum for more than twenty years of a student's life and then expect that magically he can make the proper connections between this impersonal heap of facts and the world of values which he learns Heaven knows where. If to point out to man the path to truth and enable him to grasp it is the function of the Church, then the University is and ought to be our new church.

What then is the present tumult all about? To my mind

we are in the midst of a religious war. Both among the extremely militant and among the unresisting but profoundly dissatisfied majority, there is the feeling that something is wrong with the truth which the University has been preaching. There is a conflict between two value systems, one firmly established but rarely brought out into the light for examination and another not fully formed but emerging and taking shape as the old system is challenged. Recent philosophers, for example John Dewey in his book *A Common Faith*, have argued that it would be well for humanity to draw up, without appeal to the supernatural, a set of values and beliefs to which we may commit ourselves for the simple reason that we find them good. This man-made religion is what the students are demanding, and the University is the institution which must give it shelter and ensure its survival and future growth.

II

POLARIZATION AND THE
SULLEN MAJORITY

If the 'silent majority' has not struck back, it is not for lack of provocation. Those who claim to speak for it do so without authority. It is entirely legitimate to attempt to move the lethargic to action. The art of politics consists, in large part, of splitting the centre unevenly so that the vacillating will temporarily ally themselves with one side rather than the other and the lukewarm may at least consent to check *them* if not to endorse *us*. It is not legitimate, though unfortunately it is sometimes effective, for a party leader to pose as the spokesman of the majority for the sake of convincing the world that the cause which he is promoting is already won, thereby constituting his critics as an insignificant group of disaffected who want to destroy what the rest of us have all agreed upon as good. Such is the ploy of the advertiser who plugs a book as a bestseller so that people will buy it out of fear of missing what everyone else has been reading. Of course radicals may also adopt this manœuvre, but they follow a slightly different line of argument. Their attempt is to awaken the population at large to what the radical claims to be repression of such magnitude that the victims are incapable of recognizing the extent of their oppression. The radical has at least the merit of acknowledging that his claim is a persuasive device. The truth is that the silent majority is never a single, unified group with its feelings crystallized into a definite attitude which it is waiting for some articulate spokesman to express. If this were so, it would be already

37

organized into a party. *What* majority feels this touted unanimity? The majority of apolitical Blacks certainly does not feel the same way about civil rights as the 'forgotten majority' of blue collar white workers. When what is at stake is precisely the claims of hitherto neglected minorities, the appeal to the silent majority is a device in bad faith. And what about student unrest? Is it even relevant to give serious consideration to the majority point of view if the majority consists of persons who have not been involved with a university for a long time or ever? The majority of people who have never attended a university is hardly likely to have the same point of view as those whose lives are inextricably involved with it. And among the latter, which majority is most relevant – students, faculty, alumni?

With no real evidence for the belief, which certainly could not be sustained by an appeal to history, we do nevertheless tend to assume as a truism that when the lines of polarization have been drawn taut, the correct, common-sense point of view is found somewhere in the middle. Theoretically this may be true; the trouble is that this ideal solution is rarely if ever clearly formulated. Those who fear both Scylla and Charybdis know that safety lies in finding a way between or around them, but they are incapable of *doing* anything except to drift with the current. My own experience with university faculties, and with students too – other than the activists – is that few, if any, have a well-thought-out alternative to offer as a common-sense solution. Those who make up the majority of faculty members are frankly bewildered.

The statement which I hear most often from professors interested enough to discuss the educational crisis is some version of the following: 'I approve of the students' goals and ideals but not their methods'. The speaker believes that he speaks sincerely and that what he has said is definite and means something. On occasion I have uttered these words myself, but I have come to believe that they are either untrue or meaningless and are spoken for the sake of evasion. If by 'students' the professor refers to the militant leaders who have been responsible for the more violent of campus activities, then either he is lying or he lacks that minimum of logical sense that we may rightly expect of any educator. If the professor believed, as those students do, that the goal is total revolution and the complete destruction of the existing social structure, then he would agree that revolutionary methods are called for. Better yet, they would not be necessary. For if all the faculty members who make this kind of statement did in fact approve of even most of the student demands, then the restructuring of the University would be accomplished very quickly. Administrators, many of whom have been heard to voice this same vacuity, would certainly not attempt to thwart the will of the overwhelming majority of the academic community. Assuming that the speaker means anything more than that some of his best student friends are militants, he probably wants to convey that he is sympathetic to the ideas that minorities should be given a better chance, that the war in Vietnam is a mess, that in an overcrowded university most undergraduates don't get as much good teaching as they ought to receive. If he is inclined to self-questioning, he may go a little further. He recognizes that the curriculum needs overhauling, that admission policies, examinations, and grading procedures tend to favour the conforming student and to stifle creative thought, that a disproportionate amount of required subject-matter is of little or no use to the student in his later life. In short, he admits that the system offers grounds for complaint and that the students are right in demanding something better. He recognizes that public opinion is moulded by forceful statements and that it may in turn influence administrators and legislators. He feels uneasy, even guilty, when he hears that the issue over which a student has performed an act of disobedience and been suspended or expelled by a faculty committee is one to which he had believed himself to be equally committed. His secret guilt is intensified by the suspicion that in the patterns of history the student has played the role of Bruno whereas he himself is a member of the institution maintaining the Inquisition.

At the same time it is not solely the refusal to obey the rules (usually called an infringement on the rights of others), not only the non-negotiable demands, or even the violence which prevents him from wholeheartedly upholding the radicals. He cannot support them if they want to overthrow the present system completely, not even if it is in the name of something better. Years of experience – more accurately, the study of experience – have taught him the obvious truth that it is not safe to destroy the old without knowing precisely what you will put in its place or to move forward unless you know exactly where you are going and how to get there. He is profoundly disturbed by the notion of agitating without a firm programme, of attacking without a carefully scrutinized blueprint for construction. What is still more distressing to our anguished faculty member, he finds to his embarrassment that, in the case of particular measures brought to the faculty by the students or more radical teachers, he applauds the motive behind it and yet sees that the plan proposed will simply not work. Obviously something should be done for the under-privileged minorities, but you can't just admit to the university anybody who wants to come. Look what it would do to academic standards! The role of the Negro in Western culture has been neglected, true, but it would be disproportionate and unscholarly to study his contributions in isolation. One doesn't have a course in the writings of German Americans. There is no separate Department of Australian Studies. Requirements are over-rigid, but if you don't have something, students will either earn a degree by taking all easy courses or will fall into the dangers of over-specializing or over-generalizing. Granted that grades do not accurately reflect the student's potentialities or measure the lasting value of what he has derived from the course. We cannot do away with them completely. It is necessary to provide some symbol to serve as combined threat and incentive as well as to indicate whether or not specific units of study have been satisfactorily mastered. Otherwise how could we tell when a student had completed his education and earned his diploma? And how could students' performances be compared in the competition for later honours and privileges? He discovers that he feels with the Left and votes with the Right.

If we exclude from our discussion the small minority of faculty members who have openly committed themselves to supporting the student activists and along with them the archaic remnant of those who honestly cannot see that anything is wrong with the present system except that it is less classical than the past, I think we will find that the average professor is well intentioned but distrustful, confused, and afraid.

Often the professor does not know himself exactly what is the source of his dread, confusion, and distrust. What he views as specific threats are inextricably bound up with other half-knowledged timidities and fears which he has wholly repressed. His inner landscape might be pictured as something like this: First of all, of course, he fears violence, not so much from physical cowardice or active concern lest he or others be hurt but because violence represents for him the extreme development of that irrationality which it has been his life's plan to overcome. Rationality is the cult object of his Holy of Holies, and violence comes as the ultimate enemy to rend it asunder. His feelings are like those of an ancient Israelite watching the unbeliever not only attack but prevail against the ark of the covenant. To the extent that he can believe in the possibility of a successful revolution, he is horrified at the state of affairs which would follow. He envisions himself in a totalitarian state where, if not deprived of his position entirely, he would be told what to teach and how to teach it in a university with no vestige of academic freedom. If challenged, he might admit that these fears are not very realistic. He does not honestly expect the Revolution to take place. He is very vague in his mind as to just what the radicals do want, but he knows that theoretically they oppose, they do not favour a police state. Yet his certainty that violent revolution and a totalitarian society are absolute evils is so overwhelming that the very word 'revolution' triggers off an adverse reaction to anything which the would-be revolutionists may propose. He offers an impassioned plea that revolution must be replaced by evolution, and the word play strikes an aesthetic chord. Unfortunately he inclines to think of evolution as something which comes about by methods and at a speed almost Darwinian.

He has other more hidden fears which, because they are unacknowledged, influence him more surely and cannot be reasoned away. He feels that if in some unforeseen manner 'they' and their ideas should get control, there would no longer be a place for him. He has prided himself on his knowledge, his ability to present his subject in a lucid and interesting manner, his willingness to spend extra time with bright students who show an interest in the course. He has always tried to keep abreast with what goes on in the world and made reference to it in the classroom when there was an appropriate opportunity. But he would not know how at his age to invent altogether new ways of doing things. How could he fit into the new scheme when lectures would be abolished, when ill-prepared students without prerequisites would want him to discuss contemporary affairs or perhaps simply refuse to study his subject? How could he evaluate students who would come and go as they pleased and study what and as they pleased?

Even the professor who theoretically is willing to face up to these timidities in himself and overcome them may view with dismay the loss of certain things which are essential to the system of education which he has always known. He feels that, without them, there would be chaos. He is quite right, of course, in thinking that the system could not function without them. He may fail to see that what he regards as essentials are means toward an end which is itself in question. We will hardly comfort him by telling him so. We will only plunge him into deeper gloom.

Let us assume that our professor recognizes that some of these reservations are just plain cowardice and terror of the unknown. He makes an effort to go beyond himself. He undertakes to work with some of the radicals for specific issues on which he does see eye to eye with the activists and for improvements in the system which have a reasonably good chance of being accomplished and which would at least remedy some of the evils about which almost all of the student body has been complaining. Now comes the saddest disappointment of all. His young associates either cannot or will not see that it is better to get most of what you want than to insist on everything and fail completely. They do not wish to work for those changes which will cause the least confusion, they prefer to begin with what is most fundamental and disruptive. They persist in stressing publicly the far-reaching consequences of the measure at hand and emphasizing that this is but the first step in revolution, whereas they ought to move quietly and not antagonize those who might otherwise help them. Rather than trying to avoid a confrontation, they evoke it. It finally dawns on the professor that, so far as the radicals are concerned, they may use him and his kind, but they do not want him. They distrust him, not because they think he may betray them but because they do not want to win on his terms. They are afraid that, if they gain too much faculty support, the University will be liberalized but not radicalized. The revolution will not be openly defeated but modified beyond recognition, killed by kindness, lost by default. At this stage the professor is not surprised by the apparently pointless and self-defeating acts of defiance – the defacement of property, for example, and the obscenity. He realizes that these are not without purpose and are indeed self-protective; they are acts of separation to keep the revolution total and uncompromising.

Whether our well-intentioned professor has carried out his attempt at activism objectively or merely in internal dialogue or in conversations at the Faculty Club, he is likely to fall into the pattern so perceptively depicted in a cartoon published in *The New Yorker*. A beleaguered looking citizen is trying to move ahead while trapped, as on a treadmill, in a circle where apathy gradually gives way to awareness, which leads to involvement, activism, confrontation, which in turn and just as inevitably gives way to disenchantment, to alienation, to apathy, to. . . .

Adapted from a cartoon by Lorenz in The New Yorker, 1 *February* 1969.

Theoretically one keeps moving in this circle; actually I suspect that most persons come back to apathy after one or two tries and make it their permanent residence. The professor who has traversed this road is no longer the same man. Now that he has proved that he cannot condone the approach of the militants, he sees no point in struggling by some other means to further the goals he still professes to approve. He concludes that the present system, faulty though it may be, is the best which is likely to be found. Convinced that there is no good way out, he will at best retreat more and more into the attitude that, in a period which is chaotic and irrational, the best thing for the intellectual to do is to create a small island of peace within himself and around him where he and a proven few may serve reason and the arts, enjoy the pleasures of the disciplined flesh, and wait for the rest of the world to relearn the values of rationality. He may equally well develop a cynicism about everything and everybody. Even if he continues to teach as well as he knows how, he is embittered by the suspicion that the general criticism points to his own inadequacy. He feels that the students are no longer satisfied with the best which he knows how to give them and which other students have known how to appreciate in the past. Feeling that he is misunderstood and unappreciated, he tends to be sullen and full of self-justification. None of this is conducive to improving either his own situation or that of the University as a whole.

I believe that our hypothetical professor as I have crudely portrayed him is typical of what I have called the sullen majority within the University. I suspect that, if we could poll those persons in non-university circles who have given serious thought to the problems of education, we should find that most of them, too, would profess to hold to a moderate position, 'supporting the goals but not the methods', and experiencing the same uneasiness and discomfort, traversing the same circle.

Obviously we should look for a way to break out of the circle. Where the wells are already poisoned, the only alternative is to move. Sullen passivity is not a desirable solution any more than masochism and resentment are keys to the good life. Those who believe themselves impotent are the gratuitous victims of history. The sullen majority must be persuaded that it has not adequately appraised the situation. The first step is to reconsider the polarized situation itself. What does the map of the present scene look like?

It is neither helpful nor accurate to envisage the terrain as occupied at each end by a tiny group of extremists – ultra-reactionaries on one side, socialistic radicals on the other, and a great homogeneous mass filling in between them. This is as if we were to divide the religious population into atheists, fundamentalists, and others – possible, I suppose, but hardly illuminating. I think it would be more meaningful if we were to view the present scene as split (who knows how evenly?) between traditionalists and those who feel the necessity and desirability of fundamental and far-reaching change. I believe that the basic clash here is between two value systems, but that does not mean that everyone is clearly aware of the true nature of the conflict or that he would be able to formulate with verbal precision the ideals which guide his action and his judgment. Nor is there internal unanimity on either side of the fence. Rather we have two ill-assorted clusters, made up of groups and individuals who in many cases feel a stronger hostility toward certain of their neighbours than toward most of those in the opposite camp. Nevertheless I think that it is possible for us to discern what is the nature of the two sets of values which hold each of the disparate collections together.

Let us look first at the traditionalists. Who are they? What do they hold in common besides inertia?

Many critics of the student protesters, with no intention of being unfair, will find it perfectly natural to sum up the aims of all discontented and vocal students in terms which have been proposed by the Students for a Democratic Society or by the Progressive Labour Party. They would be outraged if we were to define either the position of University faculties and administration or of the general public in a form appropriate for the followers of John Birch or even of Ayn Rand. Yet there are fellow travellers on the Right as well as on the Left, and they pose just as real a threat to the moderate liberal whether he knows it or not. In some ways the danger is still more serious, for he is more likely to fall into it with no clarion notes of revolution to warn him of what is happening.

One of the ironies of the present situation is that, whereas the young radicals denounce the University as the tool of the Establishment, there are plenty of residents in town and countryside who still see the University as the proselytizing centre of 'atheism, communism, and free love'. These people are not necessarily uneducated themselves, and, of course, many persons who are without a college education do not fall into this category. Nevertheless, in the strict sense of the word, this reactionary fringe constitutes a locus of anti-intellectualism which is different in quality but as firmly opposed to true rationality and objectivity as the most bizarre of 'hippies' or other 'dropouts'. Many of these citizens basically hate the University and all it stands for. They bitterly resent the fact that as taxpayers they must contribute to a state institution which consistently works to undermine the comfortable prejudices of those who have not even caught up with the *status quo*. They blame 'liberal' educators for all of the nation's ills. (They would include the world except that they are not accustomed to think in units larger than the nation.) As examples of this attitude, I may quote again from the paid advertisements by the local critic in my own university town.

The first is undisguised and unfocused resentment. 'What really baffles some of us is the way all academic characters who can't even run a university have all the answers for running business, the nation and the world'. The second is a bit more pointed. 'America is in its present mess not because of middle-class morality but because we have adopted the tom-cat morals and hedonistic attitudes of affluent intellectuals'. Another demonstrates the familiar phenomenon of the meeting of extremes. 'Responsible citizens should not automatically oppose SDS demands to close down colleges. Colorado might benefit – culturally and financially – if CU's Social Sciences Depts. were closed.' The last expresses openly a death wish against the University. 'One after another, university cities – Berkeley, Champaign-Urbana, Madison – are becoming narcotics and crime centres. Boulder will be next unless CU's cancerous growth is halted immediately'.[1]

It is this type of far-Right thinking which equates any criticism of American military policy with lack of patriotism, which is responsible for the decals pasted on automobiles – a picture of the American flag and the slogan, 'Love it or leave it'. Whether openly racist as in the John Birch Society or superficially egalitarian, it attacks all attempts at helping minorities by labelling them unjust 'discrimination in reverse'. When it shouts for 'law and order', it is asking for the authoritarian repression of all dissidents. I am aware that many American citizens who, weary of riots, muggings, temporary shutdowns of universities, and the disruption of business as usual, plead for law and order, do not think of themselves as supporting the reactionaries. They are middle-of-the-road, average citizens who want everyone to have a fair chance – but gradually, as a goal, not as an absolute 'must' to be instated now and regardless of the disturbance it causes.

[1] *Boulder Daily Camera*, 8 January 1968 and 10 June, 13 June, 11 August, all in 1969.

Such persons are not ill intentioned, but they should be aware that, apart from the question of the injustices which they may condone by their quiescence, their willingness to suppress all kinds of lawlessness indiscriminately without correcting the causes is effectively to support the extremists on their own side.

Someone may argue that the ultra-conservatives constitute such a small minority that they are uninfluential and are not pertinent to the issue at hand, which is to consider the kinds of values held by persons who are sincerely concerned about the future of education and who believe in the University as an institution. I will agree that reactionary critics have nothing to propose which could in any way contribute to solving the present crisis unless one subscribes to the dubious notion that the worse things get, the more sure is our hope that they will be finally changed and improved. I do not believe that such people can be safely dismissed as either numerically insignificant or irrelevant or without influence.

Richard Poirier, a professor of English and editor of *Partisan Review*, has argued that the prevalent adult reaction to the youth movement has taken on the proportions of a 'war against the young'.[1] My feeling that this claim was a bit exaggerated was considerably modified when I received in the mail one day a form letter addressing me as 'Dear Fellow American' and requesting a financial contribution to the 'STOP-NSA Committee'. The National Student Association is composed of representatives of the student governments of colleges and universities. Only institutions become members, not individuals. It is admittedly dominated by students who are left of centre and who think that the association ought to take a stand on political issues. It is by no means in the same category as the truly radical organizations like

[1] Richard Poirier, 'The War Against the Young', *The Atlantic*, October 1968, pp. 55-64.

the Students for a Democratic Society or the British Radical Student Alliance. It has certainly never been involved in subversive activity unless the verbal criticism of national policy is in itself subversion. What shocked me about the letter appealing to me to support a movement against NSA was not the fact that a move was afoot to oppose the organization but that the letterhead belonged to an Ohio Representative to the Congress of the United States. Along with his signature and impassioned denunciation of NSA were the names of forty United States senators and congressmen, presented as a 'partial list' of Congressional supporters of 'STOP-NSA'.

The full name of the STOP-NSA Committee is 'Students To Oppose Participation in the National Student Association'. This group is an *ad hoc* committee of the Young Americans for Freedom, an extreme Rightist organization, purportedly made up of students but obviously backed by powerful adult supporters. That the august members of the United States Senate and House of Representatives should stoop to such measures seems to me shameful. It is alarming as well when one looks at the specific attack which they make on NSA. According to the letter, 'a small clique of revolutionaries – a mere six per cent of the NSA delegates – continue, year after year, to ram through some of the most radical resolutions ever approved by an American student organization'. (There must be many politicians who would like to learn the trick of manipulating a legislative body when one controls only six per cent of the vote.) The shocking measures which were 'rammed through' were the following (I quote from the letter):

BLACK POWER: NSA has called for the liberation of all black people in America 'by any means necessary'.

VIETNAM: NSA has condemned 'The U.S. aggression against the people of Vietnam'.

HUAC [House Unamerican Activities Committee]: NSA has strongly urged that it be abolished.

RED CHINA: NSA has asked the U.S. to propose the admission of Red China to the UN.

With the possible exception of the vaguely sinister phrase 'by any means necessary' – taken out of context, of course – there is nothing in this list which has not been proposed thousands of times by middle-of-the-road liberals. It seems clear to me that what has frightened the legislators is not the content of the NSA proposals but the fact that a national organization of students has dared to take a strong political position. When the author of the letter goes on to say that the Committee will urge that there be 'a full scale congressional investigation into NSA's political activities', then it seems to me that we do indeed have a 'war against the young'.

My dismay at the congressman's letter was reinforced a few weeks later when I received another appeal, this time from the parent organization of STOP-NSA, Young Americans for Freedom. This was accompanied by the copy of a letter to the Executive Director from the Vice-President of the United States. It said,

My congratulations to the Young Americans for Freedom for undertaking positive programs which lend themselves to orderly participation in democracy. Your commitment and hard work give us hope that patriotism in America is not a lost virtue.

(Signed) Spiro T. Agnew

From the record of debates in state legislative assemblies, there is another incident which seems to me to merit our attention even though it is not directed toward the University problem directly. In early 1969 the Wyoming State Legislature debated a constitutional amendment which would lower the required voting age from twenty-one to nineteen. One of the Senators proposed to attach a further provision to the amendment: that nineteen and twenty year-old males should be allowed to vote only if they came to the voting booth with haircuts which in length and style conformed to military standards. 'When you accept the responsibility of a citizen, you should look like a citizen', said the Senator. He went on to explain that if nineteen-year-olds are sufficiently mature and responsible to hold the voting privilege, then 'They should look like they are. You know what these curly locks look like after they get into the service'. The Senate passed the proposal, and the amendment was scheduled to be presented to the people of the State in the elections of the following year. At least so it was reported by the Associated Press.[1] Later when I wrote to the Wyoming Secretary of State to ask for more information, I was told that 'the amendment proposed by State Senator J. W. Myers . . . was just a bit of horseplay which was picked up by the Press'.

I find in this episode the very essence of the tragi-comic which seems to characterize this age of absurdity. What particularly impresses me, however, is not only the all but incredible fact that the popularly elected representatives of the people of Wyoming, if they did not give serious consideration to this measure, were at least willing to devote time to such discussion, but something still more serious. If we look carefully, I think we will find that the underlying assumptions of the Senator's proposal are principles which would be accepted by great numbers, if not the majority of the population. Many of our sophisticated liberals would accept some of them though they would scornfully reject this extreme application as a *reductio ad absurdum*. Apart from the obvious fallacy of judging character and ability by external appearance, there are at least four implications. First, the proposal demonstrates the identification of mere

[1] Quotations from Senator J. W. Myers' remarks were printed in an Associated Press dispatch, published in the *Boulder Daily Camera*, about 7 February 1969.

convention with a moral principle. Many persons who can see that hair-style is simply a reflection of changing fashion would nevertheless argue that some other equally conventional behaviour is of the essence of moral worth – for example, conformity to the sexual code of our grandparents. Second, there is the willingness to accept the judgment of the military and to introduce it into civilian life. Third, young men of voting age (like students almost everywhere) are viewed as children who must abide by the judgments of their elders. (Note that the Senator did not have the temerity to suggest that adults of twenty-one and over should be penalized for long hair or beards.) Finally, there is imbedded here a presupposition which is hard to abstract and specify; but perhaps it is the most important of all just as it is an idea which is most frequently taken for granted as beyond the need of proof or question. This is the notion that a citizen, a responsible person, must fit a particular category which can be clearly defined and recognized. I am not speaking of conformity in the usual sense. There is something deeper here than the narrow-minded insistence that everyone must be like us. It is the conviction that both in the field of conduct and of knowledge there is easily available a clearly recognized and self-evident norm. Although I certainly do not mean to say that the Senator had all of this in mind, there is implied in his argument the belief in a scientific rationality which can guide any man of common sense to objective absolutes. It is this claim to objectivity and impersonal detachment, sometimes in good faith and sometimes in bad, which unites such diverse groups as the followers of Ayn Rand's Objectivism ('A is A'), religious fundamentalists, research scientists, the professor who writes on the final 'e' of Chaucer, and the well-intentioned liberal who will debate issues for ever but prejudge adversely any request presented during a student demonstration.

Since the concept of rationality itself is central here, let us look at it a little more closely. Perhaps it may seem that by definition there could be no misunderstanding of what we mean by rationality or reason. Actually the term raises as many problems as the concept of God. To start with, we may observe that just as has been happening with the Deity throughout the centuries, some people will conveniently identify it with their own viewpoint or desire. Two examples:

S. I. Hayakawa on one occasion was participating in a panel discussion of the student revolt. Some members of the panel had expressed the fear that the student protests might prove to have evoked a backlash which would result in a repression so severe as to be in itself a cause for further frustration and violence in the universities. Hayakawa said, 'I'm not so pessimistic. I think the forces of reason – let's not call it backlash – will begin to hold sway now.'[1] Reason for Hayakawa is simply the forces of law and order which will return us to an earlier *status quo*.

In England Anthony Lejeune, in a column called 'Violence: Tool of demagogues', argued that 'we ought to condemn not just the hard core of revolutionaries, but the whole, barbarously anti-rational cult of demonstration and agitation'. Lejeune neatly defines what he means by 'rational'. 'It would be too old-fashioned, I suppose, to suggest that colleges should require their members to behave like gentlemen: [What, I wonder, about the ladies?] but they should certainly require them to behave rationally; to talk rather than shout; to discuss rather than demonstrate; in short, to accept the 'system' – which really means the rules of civilized conduct'.[2] Reason equals the System with Hegelian finality.

[1] 'The Playboy Panel: Student Revolt', *Playboy*, September 1969, pp. 89-116 and 233-49.
[2] Anthony Lejeune, 'Violence: Tool of demagogues', *Daily Telegraph*, on the 'Opinion' page, 28 June 1968.

These are clearly examples of the misuse of the concept. The claim to objectivity is but a cloak for the rankest subjectivity, so-called rationality has become mere rationalization. Or if we wish to speak a bit more generally and to be kinder to the gentlemen in question, we may say that for them 'reason' is another name for the guiding forces of tradition. They might prefer to say that it refers to the tried and true. This is exactly what is in question, for the protesters claim that the true has yet to be tried.

More objectively, reason might be defined as that faculty which enables us to accumulate knowledge and to apply criteria by which to distinguish between fact and fiction. Theoretically I have no quarrel with this definition. In practice it has been too often interpreted in such a way as to result in narrowness of vision or out-and-out distortion of reality.

Within the University, reason and knowledge tend to be interpreted in terms wholly academic. Aesthetic 'facts' can be fitted into the realm of rational knowledge, particularly so long as one remains on the level of objective literary criticism, history of music, art history, and the like. The scientist who teaches the principle of the combustion engine still dwells in reason's sacred groves. The mechanic who diagnoses what is wrong with a particular engine and who repairs it is thought of as proceeding by something not quite the same as rational process. He possesses some other sort of skill, deemed quite illogically as being somehow allied with physical capabilities rather than mental. Such snobbism is indefensible and ridiculous, but there are more serious consequences.

Objective reason is, of course, impersonal; therefore the rational person must be detached. This is bad enough, for it immediately precludes any expression of personal commitment on the part of the teacher. Taken to its logical conclusion, it would exclude (and often it does exclude) any meaningful discussion of value judgments relative to social

E

relationships or personal fulfilment. That is, it shuns whatever is most relevant to the student's everyday life. The stress on objectivity leads naturally to the view that the product of reason is the knowledge of facts and that this knowledge can be measured. Hence the inevitable development of a grading system, of examinations for admission and for graduation, of the surreptitious introduction of gradability as a criterion of what the teacher will teach – from the first grade on up through graduate school.

Impersonality, when it moves over into the sphere of ethical ideals, becomes impartiality. No faculty member would ever admit to the lack of this virtue. Its opposite, partiality or favouritism, is perhaps the Original Sin of the academic profession. Yet here as elsewhere in human experience, the literal interpretation of the commands of conscience may in itself constitute a transgression of the spirit of the law. We may find that 'the letter killeth'. Pained and yet with smug complacency, a professor will often bestow upon a student a grade lower than he *feels* the student deserves. He will hearken only to the mathematical evidence of calculated points. He brushes aside the insistent sense that the student is better than the grade indicates, either saying that it refers to potentiality rather than to performance or distrusting it as derived solely from his own subjective liking of the quality of the student's mind. It is my conviction that often these felt discrepancies should be regarded as comparable to those small unexplained irregularities in the Newtonian calculation of the position and movements of the planets. Regarded as too rare and insignificant to point to anything but faulty application of tested theory, they proved, when thrown into question by an Einstein, to be the Achilles heel of the whole hypothetical system.

Paradoxically the emphasis on impartial objectivity has become a device in bad faith to justify an unjust and repressive philosophy of education. Comparatively few educators or parents would support an educational scheme which openly stated as its goals: to foster the ideals of the white Anglo-Saxon Protestant majority, to train docile students with good memories, to equate intelligence with verbal facility, to exclude from higher education those whose creative abilities do not fit into the prevailing pattern, to prevent the development of original ways of thinking, to weed out over a third of all college students before the attainment of an undergraduate degree. When these things have been gradually incorporated in a system whose fairness is guaranteed by the constant application of objective criteria, then it is easy to say and to make oneself believe that, if students cannot meet the standards of expectation, it is their fault and they are justly prevented from continuing further. Even if in individual cases one may feel that the failure is explainable by circumstances beyond the person's control, still the doors remain locked for one who cannot provide a key. The tears shed over this tragic situation are not necessarily those of the crocodile. It is hardly conceivable that there could exist any system or social structure in which the contingent facts of personal biography would not determine to some extent the relative success or failure of students as of everyone else. Still this does not mean that the reverse is true – that the justice of our objective criteria is so thoroughly established that it cannot be blamed for the failures of the large numbers of people who cannot meet them.

The discrepancy between the theoretical impartiality and the injustice in practice is particularly well illustrated in the United States where the national conscience has been rudely awakened apropos of ethnic minorities. As a nation we have always frowned upon the notion of an intellectual elite, and we have prided ourselves on the fact that our educational institutions are open to everyone who can meet the academic requirements. Granted that not everybody can go to the very best colleges and universities. Admittedly, too, we have not gone so far as England, for example, in offering government support to students. Yet we point out with fair accuracy that the best qualified are assured of a scholarship or fellowship, employment within the university, or at least a low-interest loan. Only very recently have we begun to show concern about indigent students who cannot meet admission requirements at academically respectable institutions. It has taken a long time for us to consider whether or not we might unlock the doors for those persons whose inadequate educations in childhood have automatically excluded them. This battle is far from won, and those who see obstacles are not always racists. The ideal of impartiality as the exact equivalent of justice is subtly refined and meticulously applied. No man of conscience would oppose effective measures for improving the elementary and secondary schools so that the problem might be dissolved. Most, though not quite all, would approve of allotting special fellowships to those who, despite their 'disadvantaged' background, had proved their superior ability sufficiently so that they might hope to compete successfully within the system after years of virtual exclusion from it. Very few indeed are willing to make concessions or to alter the University's expectations for those who have already entered. The argument runs something like this: Since reason is no respecter of persons and knowledge is the fruit of reason, the democratic ideal demands only that there should be equal opportunity to master a given curriculum. If we were to require less of the disadvantaged, this would be to treat them as inferiors. We cannot ask less of everybody, for this would transgress the sacred principle that intellectual understanding and knowing awareness are the highest human ideals and the pillar of support of the University. Therefore we must work hard to ensure that ultimately there will be equality of opportunity and everybody may realize his maximum capacity for achievement, but we cannot weaken our quest for truth and knowledge in order to take care of those who at the present state of human development cannot keep up. We must not sacrifice the person of superior achievement to the inferior even though the latter's 'inferiority' may be due to his having had no opportunity to develop his potentialities.

I do not go so far as to claim that this argument is always or entirely a cynical evasion. I agree that simply to expect less of a group or an individual is insulting condescension. And I, too, have heard a few unhappy tales of students who went to pieces psychologically because they could not perform the tasks which went with the special opportunities. Some universities have attempted to lessen the difficulties by building in a transitional semester or year, providing the special students with courses designed especially for them so as to serve as a bridge to the standard curriculum. This plan is adopted for the most laudable of motives and undoubtedly is of benefit in the existing situation. It shows also a weakness in current thought. The assumption is that those who come in with deficiencies *vis-à-vis* the established course of study are demonstrably inferior – at least in the sense of undeveloped potentiality. A better alternative would be to search for a plan by which these students might earn a degree in ways which enabled them to use their earlier experience and demonstrate the particular strengths and abilities which they had developed. To allow someone to pursue his education in a manner appropriate to him is not the same as to demand less of him. One might argue, in fact, that racism has manifested itself in our educational system in three guises. First, there was the overt denial of opportunity. Second, there was the belief that equality of opportunity meant only the invitation to everyone to compete within a set of rules which favoured the controlling majority. Finally, there is the attitude that equality demands that everybody should be helped, not only allowed, to follow all the way through on that approach to intellectual achievement which the white man in Europe and America has refined over the centuries into a model of excellence. As Simone de Beauvoir argues that for centuries 'male' has been taken as synonymous with 'human' and 'female' as the deviant or second sex, so the ideal of intelligence is equated with academic ability, and rationality with the kind of thinking that has given rise to the contemporary University.

At this point, of course, we go beyond the issue of ethnic or economic minorities. We are raising the question of whether we should hold, as the Indian saying has it, that there is one goal but many paths. Or perhaps we have gone even further than that and begun to raise the question as to whether there should be a much wider diversity and a plurality of goals. Most of such considerations must be reserved for later discussion. For the moment the point which I wish to stress is that our limited vision of what constitutes rationality may defeat the very ends of reason. For example, I suppose that most people would hold that, along with being objective, rationality is characterized by being logical. I will gladly admit that illogical reasoning, fuzzy thinking, lack of clarity, and the willingness to hold contradictory beliefs are results, ninety-nine times out of a hundred, of mental slug-gishness, intellectual laziness, or emotional prejudice. Yet there is truth, too, in Schopenhauer's remark that the person who tries to make his thought conform to the rules of formal logic is like the sound man who walks with a crutch. To reject all ambiguities may mean simply to restrict the data. Alfred Whitehead has said, 'Insistence on clarity at all costs is based on sheer superstition as to the mode in which human intelligence functions. Our reasonings grasp at straws for premises and float on gossamers for deductions'.[1] We have grown sophisticated in our knowledge of the way in which the forms and structures of our language predetermine or distort both our understanding of the problem before us and the efforts we make to solve it. We are less quick to perceive that some of our criteria for rationality are only conventional patterns of past thought and not the structure of reason itself. Nor should we forget that there is also an existential truth of the emotions which is a necessary ingredient of comprehensive human understanding. Even the impersonal neutrality of objective reason proves to be self-destructive if interpreted too universally and too narrowly. If we assume that the goal of reason is to further knowledge and to discover more truths, then certainly it is only rational to demand freedom for scientific research. But if the goal of a particular research project is to manipulate human beings so that they will follow accustomed channels (as in Huxley's *Brave New World*), then surely it is irrational not to prevent this deliberate stultification of human thought. It is non-rational not to attempt to foresee the consequences of an action one is engaged in. It is not rationality but sheer non-sense which claims that all lines of investigation are equally neutral and that detached objectivity is the only rational attitude.

Despite the allegations against them, the devotees of rationality do not intend to identify it with the memorization of facts. Nor would even the most conservative traditionalist define education as being limited to the study of the past for its own sake. Allowing for variation in details, I suspect that some such formulation as the following would be approved by all of those who wish to preserve the overall

[1] Marshall McLuhan (co-author with Quentin Fiore) quotes this sentence from Whitehead in *The Medium is the Massage*, New York, Bantam Books, 1967, p. 10; London, Penguin Press, 1967.

character of our present educational system: Truth is impersonal. Objectivity is the appropriate attitude to maintain in the pursuit of truth. Education should introduce the young person to the various branches of knowledge and instruct him more fully in a limited area which he selects as appropriate to his talents and interests. Education should both train the student for a particular vocation and enable him to appreciate the history of human culture and its achievements. Thus knowledge is both retrospective and prospective. It refers to the accumulation of already ascertained facts, but it also includes the 'know-how' for coping with situations in the future. In the pursuit of knowledge two things are important: memorizing facts (i.e. observing the evidence) and learning the objective criteria by which one evaluates them. A student attains the latter partly by committing to memory the rules which his professors and textbooks give him, principles which have been established by other people's experience. In part he learns by doing, through guided or directed experience. Finally, it is generally assumed, there is required a certain intellectual ability or talent, partly innate, partly developed by the student himself, some power which may be stimulated but which cannot be taught. Some people have more of this than others. As much as anything else, it is this which determines how far a person is able to go in the educational hierarchy and what place he will hold in society after his formal education is ended. One is judged to have completed one's education – whether in a particular course or in the institution as a whole – when one can prove that one has mastered the prescribed subject-matter, hence is master of it. The old medieval term of 'magister' was wholly appropriate. Although there are variations in the type of proof demanded, all tests include the knowledge of facts and the demonstration that, *in the manner taught*, one can apply past experience to new problems.

We are all aware, and authors from ancient times have testified to the fact that knowledge is not quite the same as wisdom. Usually the distinction is made in one of two contexts. Either we want to pay tribute to an 'uneducated' person who is rich in human understanding. Or, more rarely, we want to indicate that a person who has received recognition for formal educational achievement does not know how to deal with matters outside the academic. We tacitly assume that wisdom is a spiritual quality which has nothing to do with the intellect although it is not to be equated with the emotional either. We feel dimly that it is gained by personal experience. Evidently the experience is not that which is provided by the school system, for wisdom is at best a by-product of formal education.

In much the same way we deal with the questions of personal happiness and the individual's capacity to sustain mutually rewarding relations with other people and with society as a whole. We do not go quite so far as to say that what happens in the classroom has nothing to do with the ability to live one's life well. In a confused fashion we do affirm a connection. We assume that, while formal instruction in the traditional disciplines is neither a necessary nor a sufficient cause for the good life, still there is a positive correlation. The best way to ensure that this will be as high as possible is to do, in the most effective way possible, what we are already doing. The willingness to learn new facts, the habit of cultivating clear and objective thinking so that one may distinguish correctly between seemingly conflicting evidence and keep one's judgment unaffected by one's emotions – these are the factors which offer the best guarantee for the good life outside.

Finally we should note the relation between this philosophy of education and prevailing notions of maturity. In the lower schools we are content to distinguish as the law does and judge simply by the number of years a person has lived. Regardless of when a boy or girl reaches physiological maturity, we hold to the convention that until he is at least eighteen (most states still hold to twenty-one) his knowledge and experience are not adequate to classify him as an adult. Thus nobody is considered mature enough to determine his own life or to participate significantly in the governance of the institutions which he attends until after he has left high school. On the undergraduate and on the graduate levels, the plea that the students are still too young to be mature is a transparent fiction. Many of them are older than some of their teachers, practically all are considered adults so far as military service is concerned, most have assumed their full privileges as voting citizens. Yet until recently the doctrine that the social life of students stood in special need of authority *in loco parentis* was hardly challenged. Now the battleground has shifted to the question of the degree to which students ought to be involved in decisions pertaining to curriculum and degree requirements and the administration of the University. This is a complicated problem which should not be over-simplified. Yet one thing is eminently clear. Those members of the faculty and administration who oppose making any concession to the students' request for participation are influenced by one overriding motive – to keep the University as it has been and not to allow the possibility that students might 'put over' any revolutionary innovation. In addition to pure lethargy and the disinclination to adopt anything new, the traditionalists genuinely believe that human progress, rationality, and the established patterns of education are inextricably bound together. They see man's history as the story of the gradual triumph of civilization against barbarism, the victory of the mind over animal instincts. The obvious signs of human failure and social breakdown which the last century has witnessed appear to them as signs that vigilance must continue stronger than ever. To their elders, the young who proclaim that the evils are in the system itself appear in the guise of barbarians beginning to break through.

The values which the traditionalists wish to defend might be summed up roughly as follows: Man's highest goods are democracy, rationality, responsible freedom, the search for objective truth, impartial justice. Certain attitudes or convictions follow as corollaries. The traditionalist believes that such things as happiness and love are ultimate values, too, but his way of linking them with the other ideals is a bit paradoxical. Happiness vacillates between the status of by-product and a self-evident goal which is too abstract to exist by itself; love is almost like a superplenary grace. Neither is properly brought into the discussion of the problems of the University. It is by no means rare to hear a professor say that, if a student does not enjoy his studies, he ought not to be in the University. This seems to assume that happiness in intellectual activity is a legitimate goal. Yet there is always some suspicion attached to the idea that the students' enjoyment of their work is a proper mark for the teacher to aim at directly. If a professor is openly eager to have the class like his course, he is condemned as a seeker after popularity – perhaps scorned also as a popularizer. Another corollary is the belief that, despite little things which may be wrong here and there, the system of tested progress through a graded curriculum is, like representative democracy, the only method by which the ideal may be achieved. In short, the traditionalists may be open to modification but not to restructuring.

The spectrum of traditionalists is a broad one. It includes all of the conservatives, except possibly for a few ultralibertarians who either work spasmodically and uncomfortably with the far Left or refuse to ally themselves with anyone; it includes many but not all of those who consider themselves liberals. It ranges from the anti-intellectuals to professors who are willing to meet with students continually in an effort to find ways within the established system of satisfying the new demands or at least easing the tensions. As examples of strange bedfellows, we see here the old-fashioned fundamentalist, who resists all undermining of established institutions, and the ambitious young scientist who wishes to carry on his research objectively wherever it may lead and without raising the question of its far-range human consequences. We find the militarist but also the dovish professor of political science who believes that public debate and the voting booth remain the adequate and the only defensible means for changing the national policy. Affluent members of the business Establishment are in awkward proximity to the underpaid professor of Classics patiently ploughing through the work of earlier generations of scholars so that he may give due credit to them for ideas which he might otherwise believe to be original with him. There are students here, too, of course: those who would like to become professors themselves; bright ones with verbal facility who have received good grades from their first year at school and enjoyed praise from teachers and parents; the ambitious with an eye to becoming one of the influential in the Establishment; those who have gone to college only because it is the socially correct thing to do and who have worked out easy methods of sliding through.

Strangest of all these unlikely associations is one which I should like to consider in a little more detail. I have listed democracy as one of the ideals of traditionalists. In most circles in Europe and in America, the belief in the democratic process is constantly upheld against the socialistic leanings of the protesters. Yet if we limit ourselves to the concept of education and the notion of a university, then a strong ally of the traditionalists is the Soviet Union. Except for the kind and degree of political indoctrination which is espoused, the present educational system in Russia fits almost perfectly the ideal of many traditionalists with a social conscience.

The Soviets have gone farther than we have in the sort of programmes which American educators have only recently undertaken, projects designed to help those who otherwise either would not be admitted to the higher levels of education or who could not compete effectively anywhere in educational institutions. Our Head Start programme has developed slowly and sporadically. It attempts to give special training to selected children from underprivileged groups so that they may be more nearly on an equal basis with other children when they enter the regular public schools. The Soviet pre-school plan is much more extensive. Between the ages of three and seven most children go to state-supported pre-school institutions for six hours daily five days a week. They take part in the usual kindergarten activities – singing, dancing, drawing, game-playing. In addition, the child is introduced to the rudiments of language and arithmetic. The primary purpose, however, is not simply to start education earlier but to counteract deficiencies in home training so that every child is prepared for the later school routine. For older boys and girls who are 'disadvantaged', Moscow University maintains a preparatory school open only to children of peasants and factory workers. The Soviet Government supports a vast programme of special classes for the indigent who would not be able by themselves to qualify for college admission. Evening and correspondence courses comparable to those which have long been established in the United States are open to workers who wish to return for further education somewhat late in life. They are granted as much as a month's leave annually with pay so as to have time to study for examinations.

In their willingness to give special help to the under-privileged, the Soviets seem to defend themselves against the accusation which we here have heard so frequently: that in order to ensure that education will not be solely for a small elite, it is not enough simply to keep the doors open; we must also take special steps to guarantee that everyone knows how to find the way to them. Yet without wishing to belittle the genuine concern in Russia to provide an education for all who are able to benefit from it, I must add that it is easy to see why the student radicals have declared that their ideological connections are not with the Soviet Union; and this is not solely because of what has happened in Czechoslovakia or for any other purely political reason.

The Russian educational ideal is closer to that of Plato's *Republic*: Everyone is to be given the chance to advance as far as he is able within a clearly defined hierarchy. Knowledge is objective and measurable. Ranking of students is impartial, therefore just. There is a tight system of increasingly difficult examinations to weed out the weak students while corresponding support and privileges are given to the successful. The underlying point of view has been summed up by Professor Anatoli Ivanovich Bogomolov, head of the Methods Department for Higher Institutions in the Ministry of Education.

There is heavy competition today for the best levels of education and if you take an average, you will see that there are three applications for every opening in institutions of higher learning across the country. We can't just depend on the average student in the future. In a group, even if there is only one talented student, he must get the training his abilities deserve.[1]

This kind of thinking is elitist to the core in spite of its proletarian coating. It is similar to the goal of traditional

[1] Quoted in an article by Garven Hudgins, Associated Press Education Writer, published in the *Boulder Daily Camera*, 7 September 1969.

democracy but hardly appropriate for socialism. At best the Russian student enjoys complete equality of opportunity to fit himself into a prescribed pattern. Furthermore, the pattern is entirely academic. The Soviet Union has abandoned its earlier attempt to insist that professors and students should have experience working in fields and factories as well as in the academic disciplines. At that time candidates who had done physical labour were given preference above those who had restricted themselves to study in the classroom. Now the Ministry has decided that it cannot afford to have mental training neglected while future experts participate in the life of the workers. In recent years secondary schools and the University, too, have put more emphasis on courses in the arts and humanities. Education still leans heavily in the direction of science and technology. 'Interdisciplinary studies' for Russian educators means primarily the study of related areas which increase one's effective mastery of a given field.

In view of the constant claim that radical students are inspired, if not secretly supported, by Communists, it is interesting to see the reactions of Soviet journalists to the student movement in Europe and the United States.

A. Galkin, in an article, ' "Neocapitalism" and the Facts',[1] discusses some of the recent changes occurring in the inner structure of Capitalist countries. Among other things he points to the lowering of the average age of those who participate in the nation's economic life and the effect which this is likely to have on working conditions. Remarking that 'Young people have a greater sense of urgency when it comes to the working people's demands', and that they recognize the need of equal educational opportunity, he points approvingly to the 'class battles' which the liaison of students and workers precipitated at the time of the 1968 rebellion in

[1] A. Galkin, ' "Neocapitalism" and the Facts', *International Affairs*, published in Moscow, November 1968, pp. 31-6.

France. But obviously Galkin does not consider that either this or any other student protests are true manifestations of a Communist revolution. At most they are social upheavals which reveal the inner turmoil of neocapitalism. Referring to the common charge that these social crises are Communist inspired, Galkin states that the views and acts so labelled are typical instead of 'today's so-called ultra Left-wingers'. These pseudo-revolutionaries include Maoists, Trotskyites, and anarchists. In words which should delight Western reactionaries, Galkin complains that the students 'lack any positive platform'. He says of the non-Communist Leftists, 'Speculating on the young people's keen sense of social justice, they are trying – with some success – to move them to ill-considered and politically absurd and harmful riot action'. In reality the ultra-Leftists are 'deeply hostile to the Communists'. 'Objectively', he argues, the impulsive action of the young 'is playing into the hands of the champions of Capitalism, and in some countries the authorities, far from taking any resolute steps against the ultra-Leftists, have in fact given them a free hand and let them spread panic'. Galkin joins with those critics of the radicals who predict that their only accomplishment will be to provoke a repressive backlash.

A second article, 'Western Youth and Ideological Struggle', by K. Fyodorov,[1] reinforces this picture. Because it distinguishes more clearly the varied reasons behind the student revolt, it may also serve to lead us toward the consideration of those who challenge the current value system. The author begins by pointing out that the student protest has rightly been taken as constituting a more serious threat to society than the earlier disaffections of Hippies, Mods, Rockers, etc.

[1] K. Fyodorov, 'Western Youth and Ideological Struggle', *International Affairs*, September 1968, pp. 76-82.

This is not only because the students have on occasion resorted to violence but because they are directly engaging in politics and – with the Vietnam war as a catalyst – are challenging the entire socio-economic structure. In analysing the causes and the goals of student action, Fyodorov mentions many of the things which have by now become familiar: dissatisfaction with the oppression of minorities and with society's failure to take effective steps to eradicate poverty; disillusion at the discrepancy between the professed ideals of democracy and the pressures and repressions exerted by the Establishment; inadequate University facilities (especially on the Continent) and archaic teaching methods; lack of student freedom and participation in the governance of the University. Fyodorov claims that in seeking solutions, the students are attracted by the possibilities of some kind of socialism. Although not all of them are aware of the fact, the mainspring of their unrest is their rejection – partly for political reasons, partly on moral grounds – of the way of life which is inseparable from capitalism. He is naturally sympathetic in these observations, but he is unwilling finally to give the students his unreserved approval. Like Galkin, he finds them not truly revolutionary and certainly not Communist. He notes with regret that most of them either do not know or are unwilling to accept the ideology of Marxism-Leninism. Instead, 'Maoist views go hand in hand with neo-Trotskyism and anarchism, a chronic disease of the European petty bourgeoisie'. Especially singled out for attack is Marcuse (also criticized adversely by Galkin), who has rejected the Marxist notion that revolution must stem from and depend upon the working class. In short, he reproves the radicals for not casting their revolt in the form of a movement from Capitalism to Communism. 'Students are inclined to take revolutionary action, they are impatient and want their action to bring about instant change. On the other hand, they lack

F

revolutionary firmness, restraint and ideological hardening'. What Fyodorov objects to, in addition to the lack of commitment to Soviet-style Communism, is the issue-oriented nature of the student protests and the feeling on the part of many student groups that commitment to any ideological system is inimical to that spontaneity and freedom of action which can refuse to compromise and can insist on searching for radically new social structures and multiple novel life styles. Amusingly enough, the spokesman for world revolution, Communist style, does not want so complete a revolution as the students are demanding.

We may note one other negative aspect of Fyodorov's appraisal. He refers to archaic teaching methods and speaks deprecatingly of plans for reform (specifically in France and Italy) which 'are virtually variants of the American model and are designed to supplant higher education with syllabuses for specialists in a narrow technical field'. Just what Fyodorov means by this, I do not know and I doubt that he does. It is noteworthy that he says nothing further about the protest against the academic system as such, which, especially in America, is as live and perhaps more fundamental an issue than the specific problems of the Vietnam war and educational opportunities for minority groups. If students want to have a voice in administering the University, it is not simply out of sheer love of power but because they wish to be in a position where they can work effectively to change the style and requirements of the University. As an official spokesman of Soviet policy (I know nothing of him as an individual), Fyodorov would certainly not extend any sympathy to those who wished to undermine the dominating educational philosophy of scientific objectivity. Admittedly the Russian educational plan includes classes in political ideology. Western Europe and the United States do not, or at least not openly. I do not believe that this kind of state-controlled indoctrination is what the radical students have in mind when they speak of the need to make the curriculum relevant.

We have seen something of the range and internal variety of the groups which unite in supporting the traditional approach to education. It is time now to consider those who challenge it.

III

THE HERETICS

IN the ranks of the heretics, we cannot expect to find any wholly unified and clearly defined group of persons adhering to a single creed. We may characterize them roughly if we recall the conclusion of Jencks and Riesman. These are the students, professors, writers, and others who insist that the University must not go on preaching to the already converted, and they are convinced of the inadequacy and falsity of the faith. The traditionalists believe that the crisis in education is due primarily to the mistaken efforts of those who value neither the intellect nor the democratic ideal and that such valid complaints as have been voiced can be taken care of by specific reforms to make the system function better. The heretics put the system itself in question, both its ideals and its structure.

On the outer fringe of the traditionalists, we found an authoritarian anti-intellectualism and a thinly disguised hostility to the University as the established instrument of liberal thought. Although the qualities and motives are utterly different, we find on the far Left also a distrust of rationalism and the announced intention of radically transforming or even of closing the University, either temporarily or in perpetuity. Tom Hayden, a founder of the American Students for a Democratic Society, wrote of the leaders of the protest movement at Columbia University:

The Columbia students were . . . taking an internationalist and revolutionary view of themselves in opposition to the imperialism of the very institutions in which they have been groomed and educated. They did not even want to be included in the decision-making circles of the military-industrial complex that runs Columbia: *they want to be included only if their inclusion is a step toward transforming the university*. They want a new and independent university standing against the mainstream of American society, or they want no university at all. They are, in Fidel Castro's words, 'guerillas in the field of culture'.[1]

David Widgery, a spokesman for the Radical Student Alliance in England, stressed even more specifically the internationalist aspect of the student movement as a social revolution:

The idea that animates the political students of metropolitan Europe is a horror at the violence and hopelessness of senescent capitalism and a fierce optimism that this man-made horror must be changed by man himself. . . . Students aim to establish – or rather recover – the idea of the university as a staging post for fundamental social change outside its ivory tower, to wrest colleges away from their present role of producing obedient and politically neutral automatons and make them produce, instead, a nucleus of revolutionary intellectuals taking sides in the modern class struggle.[2]

Marxist implications are everywhere apparent in the student revolts but certainly not the Marxist-Leninism of the Soviet Union. The case of Maoism is more complicated. Mao Tse-tung is certainly one of the 'heroes' of the radical ideologists, like Fidel Castro, Che Guevara, and Frantz Fanon. But I believe that David Widgery was speaking for all but a few of the students when he declared that the replacement for modern capitalism 'most certainly will not come from Moscow or Peking'. Daniel Cohn-Bendit, leader of the French Activists in 1968, has pointed out that the Maoism which everyone talks about is not the same as the official

[1] Tom Hayden, 'Two, Three, Many Columbias', *Ramparts*, 15 June 1968, p. 40.

[2] David Widgery, 'Universities: Home of Revolution', on the 'Opinion' page of the *Daily Telegraph*, 28 June 1968.

political doctrine of China; he rejects both as being neither authoritative nor relevant for the immediate struggle in France:

> Maoism, I don't know exactly what that is! I have read some of Mao's 'things' which are very true .... But, now, Mao has become a myth. And I am not interested in talking about the myth of Mao.[1]

I think it is correct to say that the vast majority of students are searching for their own path and do not wish to accept as authoritative even those established parties to which they feel most friendly. At the same time it is true that rival groups within the SDS, at the time of the split at Chicago in the fall of 1969, were still laying claim to be the true representative of the Maoist variety of Marxism and couching their manifestoes in terms so dominated by Maoist clichés that Paul Glusman headed his report in *Ramparts*, 'More Mao Than Thou'. Inasmuch as the prevailing attitude of the activists toward Maoism is at least approving, and since China is the one large nation which is presently attempting to reconstruct its educational system in accordance with its revolutionary aims, I think it is worthwhile to take at least a glance at what has recently been going on there. I do not speak on the basis of personal observation, nor do I know of any report from a committee of observers from outside who have drawn up a perfectly objective and unbiased appraisal. Instead I am drawing from a series of articles appearing in English in periodicals published in China with official approval. Granted they are to some extent propaganda. So much the better. We are searching for guiding ideals, not preparing a sociological description. Traditionalists, too, prefer to be judged by their professed goals and honest efforts, not by their misapplications and failures.

[1] 'Interview with Daniel Cohn-Bendit', anonymous translation of an interview originally published in *Magazine Littéraire*, May 1968.

In reading these reports, I have found many similarities with the attitudes and ideas expressed by the student radicals and some striking differences. We may note, first of all, that the Chinese journalists, in contrast with the Russian commentators mentioned earlier, write of the Western student revolts with unreserved approval. To be sure, the praise is selective. The authors speak with unrestrained delight of the influence of Chairman Mao's thought and the frequency with which he is quoted in radical circles. They see the movement as launching the long awaited revolution against Capitalism. They view the struggle of the Afro-Americans with particular sympathy and, as would be expected, heartily applaud the student opposition to American imperialism in Vietnam. It is perhaps significant that, although students are commended for having initiated by themselves courses in the study of revolution and social problems, I have come across no discussion of student demands to participate in University governing boards or to be granted the more individualistic privilege of pursuing undisturbed their own life styles. Nor have I read any consideration of the principle that the University should be an institution functioning independently of the Government and on occasion actively opposing it. Perhaps these omissions are accidental or the result of my own spotty reading, but I doubt it. I think that the Chinese are reluctant to raise the question of freedom of dissent, whether by the individual or by an institution.[1]

Looking first at the things of which those in the Western youth movement would approve, I am immediately struck by the guiding slogan which appears everywhere in these discussions: 'struggle-criticism-transformation'. Perhaps someone might argue that this verbal triad would apply equally

[1] My information has been drawn from articles appearing throughout 1968 and 1969 in three journals, *Peking Journal*, *China Reconstructs*, *China Pictorial*, all published in Peking.

well to any revolutionary programme. Admitted. Nevertheless it denotes accurately the spirit of the Chinese programme, and it might serve equally well to sum up the intent of the Western radicals; that is, first the struggle to be listened to and taken seriously, then the negative procedure of wiping out the specific evils of the system, finally the constructive transformation of society. The emphasis is on action and change. The assumption is that the resolution to restructure has already been made; we are in process of implementing our decision. The slogan is the opposite of the traditionalist spirit, which might be phrased as 'defend, discuss, absorb'.

If the University is to be one of the instruments for social change, it must itself be transformed beyond recognition. There is admittedly a strong negative element here as well as a positive one.

Chairman Mao teaches us: 'There is no construction without destruction. Destruction means criticism and repudiation; it means revolution. It involves reasoning things out, which is construction. Put destruction first, and in the process you have construction'.[1]

Another quotation from Mao puts it still more negatively. 'Before a brand-new social system can be built on the site of the old, the site must first be swept clean'.[2] These statements express clearly the attitude of many of the young Western radicals – that there are two steps to be taken and that the first consists of getting rid of what you know to be wrong. Put unkindly, it sums up the complaint of their sharpest critics: 'They want to tear down the old without having anything to put into its place'.

Whatever one may think of what has been happening in China, destruction of what existed earlier has been inextric-

[1] *Peking Review*, 13 December 1968, p. 20.
[2] *Peking Review*, 17 May 1968, p. 12.

ably bound up with the installation of something new. Mao Tse-tung's overhaul of education has ostensibly put youth in the forefront. 'The young people are the most active and vital force in society. They are the most eager to learn and the least conservative in their thinking. This is especially so in the era of socialism'.[1] From one point of view, it may truthfully be said that it has been the young revolutionaries who have conducted the revolution in education, literally taking the University into the fields and factories. The liaison with the workers, which (except for a brief period in France and Italy) Western radical students have cherished as a goal more than an actuality, is a reality in China. In fact, the intellectual has become a helper or follower in a manner suggesting the common relation of left-wing Whites to militant Blacks. Mao stated in a public speech, 'The dividing line between revolutionary intellectuals and non-revolutionary or counter-revolutionary intellectuals is whether or not they are willing to integrate themselves with the workers and peasants and actually do so'.[2] Those SDS workers who worked manually and politically in factories during their summer vacations would undoubtedly be sympathetic with this statement. I am not quite sure that they would want to go quite so far as Chinese university students in giving up their own leadership. Titles of selected articles suggest the extent of the dominance of the hitherto uneducated. 'The Working Class Must Exercise Leadership in Everything'; 'Poor and Lower Middle Peasants Manage Schools'; 'Workers, Mao Tse-tung's Thought Propaganda Teams, Lead Proletarian Revolution in Education'; 'Working Class Enters Universities to Lead the Revolution'; 'Led by the Working Class, New Peking University Advances Courageously'; 'The Lowly Are Most Intelligent'.

What does all of this involve? In part it is, at least in

[1] *Peking Review*, 31 May 1968, p. 3.　　　　[2] Ibid., p. 4.

intention, a very positive plan for breaking down the walls which have separated the University from the rest of society. Professors and students of engineering join with workmen in the manual labour of dredging a river. Factory workers come to the University to share their practical experience with students studying the theoretical aspects of technology. Young physicians who have just earned their degrees and advanced medical students go out into the countryside to train peasants in practical methods of caring for the sick or of preventing disease; these trainees go on to communicate the skills to others. Partly, too, the emphasis is on political indoctrination. Propaganda or thought control, the cynical will say. Idealists will see it rather as the necessary stage of a society in crisis which is consciously remaking itself. Be that as it may, a large proportion of time and effort is devoted to discussions and instruction in revolutionary thought. The avowed intention is that the workers should take the initiative in criticizing all aspects of the educational system so that elitism and academicism are eliminated once and for all. Emphasis is given to training for the practical aspects of living rather than to strictly academic subjects. Along with making it possible for all to attend communal schools, Mao has seen fit to shorten the length of time to which the average person must go in order to be educated. A child may enter at the age of six or seven and graduate from 'senior middle school' when he is fifteen or sixteen.

This is precisely a suitable age to begin taking part in farm work. After doing farm work for a few years and gaining practical experience, some can be selected to go to university. Relatively speaking, such a period of schooling conforms to actual conditions in the countryside and facilitates universal education. It is greatly welcomed by the poor and lower middle peasants.[1]

[1] *China Pictorial*, December 1968, pp. 30-1.

It would be wrong to think that this programme smacks of the old ideal of training the rich and superior in universities and sending the poor and inferior to vocational schools. If any group is threatened, it is the old-style academician. There is, in fact, a pronounced anti-intellectual bias which permeates all of this effort at the expansion and restructuring of education. 'Some intellectuals who are self-proclaimed "proletarian revolutionaries" oppose the workers whenever the working class touches on the interests of their tiny "independent kingdoms"'.[1] This kind of criticism comes dangerously close to opposing freedom of thought as well as cutting off the scholar's privilege of devoting himself to the pursuit of knowledge for its own sake. I think the threat is real though in fairness it should be added that such reproaches are directed specifically against the supporters of 'China's Krushchov' (Liu Shao-chi) who, from the point of view of Mao and his supporters, had temporarily halted the full development of the revolution. The passage which I have just quoted is followed by a more general denunciation.

Away with your ugly, bourgeois intellectual airs! There are two kinds of education: bourgeois education and proletarian education. What you 'understand' is the pseudo-knowledge of the bourgeoisie. Those who teach science and engineering do not know how to operate or repair machines; those who teach literature do not know how to write essays; those who teach agricultural chemistry do not know how to use fertilizer. Aren't such laughing-stocks to be found everywhere? The proletarian educational system under which theory and practice accord with each other can be gradually brought into being only if the proletariat takes a direct part.

What of the professors in all of this? Teng Wen-yu, identified as a 'technician of the Fushun Petroleum Research Centre under the Ministry of Petroleum Industry', links the

[1] Yao Wen-yuan, 'The Working Class Must Exercise Leadership in Everything', *China Reconstructs*, November 1968, pp. 4-8.

new appreciation of the workers with Mao's programme for the 're-education of the intellectuals'.

> Our great leader Chairman Mao has pointed out: 'I came to feel that compared with the workers and peasants the unremoulded intellectuals were not clean and that ... the workers and peasants were the cleanest people. ...' I now recognize that there is dirt in the minds of intellectuals like me, though in appearance our hands are not soiled and our feet not smeared with cow-dung. I am also gaining a deeper understanding of the fact that intellectuals must be re-educated by the working class precisely because the bourgeois and petty-bourgeois ideas and sentiments we absorbed from the old schools and colleges should undergo a change. Intellectuals cannot serve the workers and peasants well if they do not change and remould their thinking and their feelings, if they do not remould their ideology and make it as clean as that of the workers.[1]

Another section of this article bears the caption, 'It is the Working Class, Not Intellectuals Who Consider Themselves "Learned", That Really Possesses Knowledge'. On the whole, these discussions from China speak very optimistically of the way in which university professors have welcomed their own re-education or at least consented to be 'remoulded' after being reasoned with in conversations with the already converted. Apparently only a minority proved to be hopeless, and we are not informed as to what happened to this recalcitrant few except that they could no longer continue on in their same posts to block the national will.

There is much in these articles which sounds like what the radical students have been urging. We find the familiar insistence that what is taught must be relevant to the needs of a society in crisis, a special concern for the rights and for the values of hitherto repressed groups. There is a tendency to identify intellectual with academic and to condemn both in

[1] Teng Wen-yu, 'Honestly Receive Re-Education by the Working Class', *Peking Review*, 1 August 1969, pp. 15-17.

favour of a concept of education which would stress the practical. We meet the absolute refusal to subject all students to a kind of learning which is thought to be appropriate only for the few who genuinely wish to be scholars. University community and the community outside are scarcely distinguishable. (I am reminded here of a statement which has been attributed to Fidel Castro to the effect that in Cuba universities would eventually disappear since university training will be provided 'in each factory, each agricultural unit, each hospital and each school. The country will practically be a university'.[1]) I do not myself believe that in the process of de-academicizing the University in the interests of social progress, very many of the Western radicals would go as far as to dismiss those professors who insisted on teaching esoteric subject-matter in their accustomed manner. I think that the students would probably restrict themselves to removing requirements of compulsory attendance and the threat of reprisal through grades. On the other hand, I recall reading a quotation from a young professor at Princeton, spoken how seriously I do not know. 'For me, the students are the only really viable political entity. . . . Older faculty are ineducable when it comes to the revolution, the movement. They won't be shot, you know; a little island will be found for them some place.[2] The question of the degree to which freedom of dissent would be allowed in the new society which the radicals would like to found is a ticklish one. In China it is no longer a problem.

In the Chinese articles as in discussions by Western radicals, there is much mention of 'classes in revolution'. At times this seems to refer to the genuine study of specific social problems so as to understand them and discover appropriate solutions.

[1] Associated Press Dispatch from Havana, published in *Boulder Daily Camera*, 9 December 1968.

[2] Charles W. Wheatley, quoted in *Time*, 5 January 1970, p. 39.

On other occasions it means simply the study of the works of
Mao or direct political indoctrination. I have never been quite
sure what students in our hemisphere mean by their references
to 'classes in revolution'. I suspect that they, too, envision
more than one kind. Possibly some classes would discuss and
criticize relevant social theories, some would analyse community and national problems, others would work out projects
in connection with the specific needs of the local community.

Perhaps the most striking parallel between these circles
of East and West is the fundamental assumption that in the
new-born society each individual will best fulfil himself
within the community by working for the common good
of all. In China the ideal has been formulated in the writings
of Mao. Western youth has not yet spelled out its philosophy
in a total theoretical system, but the communal ideal will
clearly be at the heart of it. The old-fashioned ideal of
pluralism is a thing of the past. Nevertheless this point, if no
other, would force us to recognize that, along with the
similarity of views, there are marked differences between
Maoism and the attitude of all, or at least the majority of even
the most activist of Western students.

Despite the influence of Maoist thought on European and
American students and the reverence which they feel for him,
I doubt that we could find a single one, certainly not more
than a handful, who would be willing for any man to receive
the institutionalized charisma which has been bestowed upon
Mao in China. The *Peking Review* reports:

The first thing the poor and lower-middle peasants did was to
arm the teachers and students with Mao Tse-tung's thought, and to
put Mao Tse-tung's thought in occupation of the classrooms and in
command of everything. In the past the first words the students said
on their arrival at the schools were 'Goodmorning, teacher', now
their first words are: 'We wish Chairman Mao a long, long life!'[1]

[1] *Peking Review*, 8 November 1968, p. 14.

Generally speaking, I have disdain for those who can see only similarity and no differences between fascism and any kind of proletarian revolution, but I confess that the pupils' greeting is horribly reminiscent of the Nazi salutation, 'Heil Hitler'. The Chinese writer goes on to explain that the first period of every day is devoted to the reading of Mao's works, an exercise called the 'daily reading'. This reminds us rather of the traditional daily reading from the Bible in public schools in the United States, finally declared unconstitutional by the Supreme Court. But more is involved here than the question of the authority of a single political leader.

The students' movement has been characterized from the beginning by a reluctance to ally itself with any established party or to organize itself into a new party. It has been unwilling to define itself in terms borrowed from the political theory of any one person or group, and it has resisted the temptation to crystallize its own philosophy in any final form. Even while avowing that its aim is the restructuring of education and of society as a whole, the leaders of the movement have remained to some degree 'issue oriented'. Daniel Cohn-Bendit described the position very clearly:

When we conducted very precise struggles – against sexual repression, in favour of the liberty of political expression, in favour of politicizing of the student milieu – we ran up against total repression, up until the present paroxysm. Starting from that, we now have to develop a new strategy of politicizing in order to continue posing political problems. And in posing these political problems, precise objectives will reveal themselves to us within the universities and, more generally, within the educational system, and outside, in relation to the working class.[1]

The young radical wants to make a revolution somewhat in the manner of an artist painting; that is, he has in mind a general idea of the composition and overall quality at which

[1] 'Interview with Cohn-Bendit', pp. 96-7.

he is aiming, but the particular relation of details and final unity will emerge in the process of creation, as a product aimed at but never fully conceived until it has been completed. By comparison (though this is not entirely fair) the Maoist revolution resembles the construction of an engineering project in strict accordance with a blueprint.

Another striking difference revolves around the question of strongly centralized control versus decentralization. Yao Wen-yuan says:

> The theory of 'many centres', that is, the theory of 'no centre', mountain-stronghold mentality, sectarianism and other reactionary bourgeois trends undermining working-class leadership must be opposed. . . . All units should accept leadership by the revolutionary committees. It is impermissible to allow in our country the existence of any 'independent kingdom', big or small, which is counter-posed to Chairman Mao's proletarian headquarters.[1]

The radicals are, of course, notoriously disunited, sometimes to their own detriment. This is not due to the emergence of factions within a unified organization but to the fact that the radicals have on principle worked by means of *ad hoc* alliances of independent groups. Cohn-Bendit, once again, sums up the situation concisely. 'I am against the organizational method of democratic centralism and for organizational federalism, for autonomous, federated groups that act together, but always maintain their autonomy'. Here he is speaking of the method best suited for instituting change. But the idea of decentralization as one of the goals of revolution is upheld by many of the radicals, especially in the United States.

One of the puzzling and controversial aspects of the youth movement is the appearance from time to time and place to place of what can only be called libertarianism. There is

---

[1] Yao Wen-yuan, op. cit., p. 6.

no unanimity with respect to the personal freedom of the individual. For the Progressive Labour Party, which at one time attempted to dominate the SDS, individualism is a term inseparably tainted with the connotations of irresponsible capitalism and *laissez-faire*. It might be defined as the will and privilege to go one's own way without being accountable to others. Yet in many activist circles one will be told that the mainspring of the student revolution is the desire to liberate all of the population from a repressive system which presently enslaves man without his even being conscious of his loss of freedom. This captivity of the human spirit, as contrasted with overt economic or political oppression, is the theme of Herbert Marcuse's *One Dimensional Man*, a book which has been variously treated as revelation or as a treacherous revisionism, depending on which revolutionary circles one inhabits. One of the constantly reiterated demands of the students has been that they should be allowed to live by their own value systems, including everything from clothing and hair styles to sexual *mores* and the use of drugs. Freedom to 'do your own thing' is not necessarily in conflict with social responsibility, but the proper relation between the two certainly needs a lot more discussion and is perhaps the biggest single problem ahead of the young radicals. They should be given credit for recognizing that concerned members of society ought to search for a new concept of individualism and personal freedom which is compatible with the values of responsible community. Meanwhile we may note an existing tension in radical thought which may be symbolized by the continued popularity of Nietzsche, on the one hand, and Mao Tse-tung on the other. On this side, the glorification of Dionysus and self-fulfilment through intense experience; on that side, the condemnation of any search for fame or personal distinction.

Finally we may note another opposition in Western and

G

Eastern radical thought. Here we have a revolt against detachment and objectivity. There Mao reproaches intellectuals for their subjectivity; Yao Wen-yuan declares proudly, 'Everything that exists objectively can be known'. Granted that the difference is explained by the historical situation, nevertheless the fact remains that Western students are revolting against the domination of technology and reaffirming the values of mysticism, feeling, the religious and the personal encounter. In China the threefold revolutionary movement embraces 'class struggle, the struggle for production, scientific experiment'. It is ironic to hear the constant denunciation of the bond between the Western university and the military-industrial complex and then, in the pages of *China Pictorial*, to read about three-man committees which direct the work of reconstruction in the universities – committees made up of a factory worker, a student or young faculty activist, and an officer from the revolutionary army.

I have felt that it was worth our while to look, albeit superficially, at these reports from China. I must add, however, that while I am personally dismayed at certain things which are happening, my intention has not been to stress only the negative aspects. Furthermore, although I have indicated certain respects in which I think that the realities in China are incompatible with the ideals of Western radicals, there are two pertinent observations which should be made. First, students who profess admiration for Maoism have no desire to imitate the Chinese revolution in detail; they are well aware that our specific problems are different and call for other solutions. What they admire is the spirit and overall purpose of the social revolution. Second, regardless of one's own prejudices and preferences, one must agree that at least in theory certain of these aims are transferable to American and European societies. I refer especially to three things: (1) the possibility of deliberately engaging ourselves in a prolonged period of restructuring our schools and universities, something which can be accomplished only if we accept the view that we are in a period of social crisis and that drastic re-ordering is necessary; (2) the intermeshing of University and the outside community; (3) the absolute destruction of the vestiges of elitism which are the academic equivalent to social injustice in the world at large.

The student movement may be said to have both an external and an internal aspect. While most of the young people who are sufficiently discontent with the *status quo* to advocate reform will be working on both fronts, this is not true of all. Some of both Blacks and Whites will be more concerned to ensure that all have a realistic opportunity to enter the University than they will be to change the nature of its offerings. Not every youth who fights for student participation in administering the University and in planning the curriculum is ardently devoted to politicizing the workers. The question of what constitutes the best kind of formal education within an institution and the problem of guaranteeing a just society are formally separate. In practice it is almost impossible to solve one without the other.

I have been particularly interested in two attempts to sum up the student accusations. The first is by Ivan Illich, who, as we noted earlier, believes that the age of the School is drawing to a close. Illich claims that we have confused education with 'scholarization'. That the process must be halted is recognized 'in the Third World, the ghettos, the universities'.

In the Third World, scholarization effectively discriminates against the majorities and discourages the self-educated. Many Blacks in the ghettoes maintain that the School is an instrument for 'whitening'. Finally, groups in the forefront of the student world tell us that youth is bored at school, wastes its time there, is alienated there. These statements no doubt border on caricature, but the academic tabu makes it very difficult to conduct an objective investigation of the truth of these accusations.[1]

The second summation aims not at analysing the origins of the complaints but at combining them into a total picture. It was offered by Martin Meyerson, former President of the State University of New York at Buffalo, who reminded fellow panel members that 'we will ignore this rhetoric of the angry young at our peril'.

The rhetoric proceeds in many fashions: Science and technological research presumably are geared to immoral ends. They claim that we engage in these immoral activities and reward only those who have publications rather than teaching skills. They go further and condemn our humanistic bias as the bias of an elitist group concerned with the past, concerned with kinds of humanism that may have been appropriate to the class structure of the Italian Renaissance, but hardly to the contemporary world. They claim it is the bias of the verbal against the sensual; a bias that ignores the visual, the auditory, the other senses. . . . Substantial numbers of students – and not just the most politicized – have a deep concern with an educational experience that they find very wanting.[2]

These quotations from Illich and Meyerson illustrate the external and internal aspects of the protest and point up their inextricability. Some members of the extreme Left, whose goal is total social revolution, have on occasion gone so far as to acknowledge that they attacked the University first only

[1] Ivan Illich, op. cit., p. 678. I have not seen the original Spanish of the article which was published in a French translation in *Les Temps modernes*. The French 'scolarisation' is a coined term like its English cognate.

[2] Martin Meyerson, participant in a Conference on Higher Education in Industrial Societies, sponsored by the American Academy of Arts and Sciences. The report of the conference appeared in *Daedalus*, Fall 1969, pp. 1157-1223.

as a matter of expediency because it was the institution most vulnerable to attack. Ironically, its vulnerability was not due to its being more obviously in the wrong or because it was the most glaring example of social injustice. Quite the contrary. Immanuel Wallerstein has pointed out that the University has always had a bifurcated view of its relation to society. It recognizes that it is expected to serve the ends of the specific society which supports it; that is, to train the young to live effectively in the particular milieu into which they will enter after graduation. In another sense it owes its allegiance to the transcendent community of scholars and pursuers of truth who affirm their association across the ages and all national boundaries.[1] This second view requires that its goal is to cherish and to live by an ideal which cannot be defended by an appeal either to expediency or to the policies of contemporary government. The acknowledged aim of serving all mankind and the habit ingrained in intellectuals of feeling that they must be able to justify their position in rational argument render them peculiarly open both to public demands for such justification and to self-questioning.

Yet even as the radicals speak of making the University an instrument for social reform, they are concerned about it as an end, not just as a means. Or more accurately, they are interested in the kind of social instrument it will be in the new society, not merely in its effectiveness in helping to bring that society into existence. Possibly educational institutions would, in their expectation, be transformed beyond recognition, but the problem of what is taught to whom and how cannot be ignored. On the other hand, the problem of the internal reform of the University involves the whole question of our philosophy of education. We must decide anew what knowledge is and how it should be taught. We are led

[1] Immanuel Wallerstein, *University in Turmoil: The Politics of Change*, New York, Atheneum, 1969, pp. 4-5.

inevitably to the discussion of the kind of society for which we are educating. At either end we are brought back to the underlying conflict of values.

If we try to formulate the central value system which holds the Left together in spirit, no matter how great the difference in specific details of goals and methods, I think we will find that it includes the following:

In the first place, there is the conviction that most people live a repressed life which is either empty or filled with suffering, that a better – by which they mean a more deeply satisfying and happier existence – is possible and that the University should exert every effort to ensure that the opportunity to achieve it is provided for everyone. This ideal is a complex one and involves several quite different notions. To start with, I should like to emphasize its positive aspect. I am convinced that in the early and more negative days of the Beatniks and other groups who were hostile to society but who saw no solution except personally to withdraw from it, a prime cause was the loss of the belief in the possibility of human happiness. Youthful rebels of the kind described in the Kerouac novels saw the hollowness of what their parents called happiness just as they saw the falsity of their elders' lip service to the old Puritan ethic. But instead of concluding that the ideal of the older generation was not for them and searching for something to replace it, they tended to accept the judgment that happiness was equated with middle-class contentment, hence to conclude that any form of happiness was impossible for themselves. This was the period when I encountered the most distressing and hopeless cases during all of my teaching career – students who could not conceive that any goal at all was worth working for or that any state of being could be intrinsically rewarding. The mood is akin, of course, to the lament, 'There are no more noble causes', to which Osborne's character gave vent in *Look Back in Anger*. All of that has changed now. The spirit of the student movement, if not quite utopian, is exuberant. It assumes that happiness can be realized just as it believes in the possibility of a world without war or poverty. The achievement of both depends on a reconstruction of social structures, one which will transform our inward attitudes as well as our institutions and laws.

The absolute equality of man is a corollary ideal, but this is more than a restatement of the principle of democracy – although as happens in any revival, some radicals have claimed to be merely going back to the never-honoured promises of the United States Constitution. It includes the principle of reparative discrimination, that is, offering special favours and opportunities to those whose poverty or colour or ethnic background have held them back in normal competition within the present order. It has given rise to the Women's Liberation Front as well, a neo-feminist movement which seeks to actualize the theoretical equality of men and women just as civil rights workers have challenged the doctrine of 'separate but equal' and fought to unmask token integration. This organization illustrates another aspect of the new notion of human equality. As with all of the youth organizations, those agitating for the liberation of women are not closely united but work in splinter groups which are quite different from one another. Thus some women's groups concentrate on ways to ensure equality in job opportunities and salaries. Others work to change what they regard as attitudes and customs which have degraded woman into a mere sex object or, at best, a dependent being – including everything from Madison Avenue advertising and elaborate cosmetics to the law that a wife must assume her husband's name, the institution of marriage, and the customary distribution of household responsibilities. Still others take a totally different tack. Declaring that there really is a distinctively feminine approach to reality, even in matters where sex is not directly involved, they lay claim to a special kind of knowledge, intuition, and feeling, declared to be equally valid with 'masculine' rationality and capable of arriving at kinds of truth which are attainable in no other way. Taken to its logical but non-rational conclusion, this position ends up by reaffirming not only the old values of mysticism but the powers of magic and witchcraft. Some of the leading Witches of the movement seem actually to believe in these powers of woman as earth mother; others find in the attendant rites a satisfying ritual. In either case it is startling in the second half of the century to witness a ceremony which formally and publicly puts a hex on the Pentagon and almost as surprising to have feminism presented in the guise of a doctrine that the sexes are different but equal.[1]

However mistaken one may find this extreme manifestation, there are two ideas involved here which appear in less bizarre contexts elsewhere in the movement. First is the belief that the whole cluster of givens and absolutes, in the sphere of knowledge and in the realm of values, represents a partial and one-sided view, that it is one kind of organization of reality and not reality itself. From the point of view of the protesters, so-called objective knowledge and impersonal democratic education are inextricably bound up with the particular values of the White, the male, the Puritan ethic, nationalism, and the scholarly specialist. The University, like the Church in recent times, should be subjected to a process of demythification (Illich prefers the term descholarization). What should be put in its place? Here there is no unanimity. At times student leaders stress the desirability of a new unified

[1] To my knowledge, the only documented case of rites of exorcism involving the Pentagon has been described by Norman Mailer in *The Armies of the Night*. Performers here were male groups. Irrationality is no respecter of sexes.

social vision to which all might subscribe and then work together for the common good. This is clearly related to the goal of social revolution, one manifestation of which we have seen in Maoism. Ivan Illich would go so far as to do away with the school entirely. Ewart Brown, student-body president at Howard University and leader of Howard dissents, is more conservative and objects primarily to the University's training of specialists to keep the established economy running. 'We've got to produce a generation of generalists – men and women who, whatever their major fields of interest, also understand the problems of the world and have the will and compassion and the imagination to help solve them'.[1] At other times the emphasis is on diversity. Edgar Friedenberg, identified as an 'anti-establishment educational theorist' says:

> The university is not a factory and shouldn't manufacture a 'product' – even a humane, socially committed product. It shouldn't produce revolutionaries or 'responsible citizens' or any other *types*. If we must use the metaphor of production, the students should be their own manufacturers and create the selves they want to be.[2]

Along with the 'purging' of the educational ideal, we find a certain neo-primitivism. This may manifest itself simply in the rejection of the life of affluence and of the 'gospel of work', in which case it may give rise to experimentation with new ways of communal living or to the search for a closer relation to nature. At times it takes on the form of anti-intellectualism. When this is something more than pure escape into irrationality, it may be expressed in the claim that there are legitimate forms of knowledge which are neither scientific nor academic and that educators are at fault in excluding them. Others conclude that only snobbism sets ultimate value on university education and that perhaps the best education is to be achieved

[1] 'The Playboy Panel: Student Revolt', op. cit., p. 242.   [2] Idem.

outside all institutions. An attempt to combine both these points of view results in the demand that the University should provide an education which – unlike the present offerings – is appropriate for other than would-be scientists and future scholars. Throughout the movement there is much talk of the necessity of recognizing that love must be combined with justice and the insistence that in some way the University must take the lead in educating students in the ways of founding and living in a world based on love and faith in the possibility of a creative life and happiness for all.

When it comes to the question of implementing the revolution in education, there is as wide a divergence in point of view as we saw among the traditionalists. A few militants think that only a violent revolution can wipe the slate clean enough so that anything significantly new can emerge. Others whose ultimate goals are just as far-reaching will stop short this side of violence as a method, either out of moral conviction or because they do not believe it is efficacious. In the minds of some, the talk of the coming revolution is seen as an excuse for present inaction. They will quote Simone Weil's aphorism, 'Revolution is the opiate of the people'.[1] Almost all are willing to adopt strikes, sit-downs, mass demonstrations, and other non-violent actions which go beyond the traditional parliamentary forms of debate. It is approval of this kind of militancy which ultimately separates the well-intentioned traditionalist who thinks he is open to gradual orderly change from men like Harold Taylor and Paul Goodman, who are not willing to abandon the system entirely but do feel that extraordinary methods are justified in awakening us to the need of a thorough overhauling of the University as the key institution for social change.

Among those who criticize the radicals for reasons other

[1] I first heard this remark from Jeremy Brecher at the Institute for Policy Studies at Washington, D.C.

than their own reluctance to have their comfortable nooks in the *status quo* thrown into jeopardy, three objections are voiced most frequently. First, the rebellious students are inconsistent in their complaints and demands; they do not really know what they want. Second, they try to tear down without any plan for replacing what they will have destroyed. Third, they condone violence and are far more intolerant of dissent than the Establishment which they attack as repressive. These are serious charges. Do they justify the refusal of the sullen majority to listen any longer to what is being shouted at them?

First, what about the charge of inconsistency? In part this is the result, as I have tried to show, of disunity among the heretics themselves. To the extent that this is true, our task is obviously to try to ascertain which is the prevalent view and which belongs to a small minority which would be considered extremist even among the radicals. No revolution has ever existed without its lunatic fringe. It is also true, however, that some of the more generally held goals of the student dissidents seem to be mutually opposed. For example, the aim to reconstruct society so as to eliminate racism and other forms of discrimination is not necessarily consistent with the plea for the principle of self-determination for neighbourhoods and small groups and freedom from centralized Big Government. In the academic sphere, there is a parallel problem. Equality of educational opportunity appears to require that, from the child's earliest years, he should be offered exactly the same kind of schooling as is available for everyone else. How can this be done without instituting exactly the pressure for conformity against which the entire youthful generation is rebelling? In another area we find students complaining that senior professors do little or no teaching and leave too large a proportion of undergraduate course work to be handled by graduate teaching assistants.

Side by side with this complaint is the suggestion that many students or experts from outside without university degrees could do effective teaching and should be allowed to do so. The plea for more personal encounters with professors is made along with the demand for the abolition of all vestiges of the doctrine of *in loco parentis*. The University is simultaneously reproached for its impersonality and for its refusal to let the student determine his career without interference. At the same time that they ask that grades be abolished, some students have set up the practice of grading professors by a mathematical scale and publishing the results. So it goes, and I do not deny that, in a period of unrest, much of the voiced discontent may resemble the plaints of a man who is ill but unable to effect an adequate self-diagnosis, let alone prescribe a proper cure.

Yet in all fairness, two observations should be made. First, inconsistency is by no means limited to the side of the radicals. One could point, for example, to the odd practices of admissions offices at certain universities where competition for entrance is keenest. They require that all incoming students should be 'well-rounded' in order to turn them into specialists as rapidly as possible. High grades are a *sine qua non* despite the fact that there has been proved to be very little positive relation between the ranking of entering students and their later performance. The correlation between scholastic achievement in college and success in a post-college career is even more conspicuously lacking. As for the fact that an alarmingly high percentage of the carefully screened students drop out before earning their degrees, this is troublesome to academic authorities who wonder what is wrong with the cream of American youth and search for psychological reasons to explain the failure of those who have been selected for intellectual excellence. It seldom if ever occurs to the authorities that the fault might lie in what has been offered rather than in the young men and women who have been unable or unwilling to receive it. More important than the *tu quoque* defence is the fact that in any movement for total reform, there are bound to be conflicting demands just as there are polarized needs within a single individual. The approved method of satisfying the conflicting claims of individual freedoms in society has usually been a compromise which attempts to allot to each person the maximum privilege which he can enjoy without infringing upon the comparable right of every other. In theory there is nothing wrong with this principle. In practice the result has often been a too easily reached decision to impose an equal restriction on everyone rather than to provide ways in which greater deviance and diversity might be allowed without either repression or mutual destruction. Revolt against this kind of life-killing compromise was an initial impetus for the student movement.

The accusation that student activists have no positive programme seems to me the most unfair of all the taunts levelled against them. With regard to particular issues, their demands have been specific and emphatic – especially in matters involving programmes for minority groups, University acceptance of defence contracts, changes in degree requirements, and student participation on administrative and faculty committees. It is not the vagueness of student proposals which has harassed the life of administrators in recent months, and it would be hard to prove that they were all intrinsically negative. It is true that the proponents of revolution or total restructuring have not presented a detailed blueprint for the future. Is it really reasonable to expect them to do so? To my mind, the most valuable quality of an approach like that of Cohn-Bendit is what I should like to call measured transcendence. This is quite different from the old-fashioned utopianism which assumed that a carefully worked-out plan could be imposed upon society in such a way as to solve all existing difficulties without creating new ones. It is equally opposed, of course, to gradualism, which would institute reform slowly so that one would never at any point experience a clear disruption with the past or even a serious disturbance of the present. Except for the small minority of students committed to a political theory already established, the radical students really mean it when they say that they are working for the kind of liberation which will bring something truly new into the world. They have a clear enough picture of the quality and values and overall character of the society to-be so that they can see clearly the obstacles which stand in the way as well as certain positive steps which must be taken in the desired direction. Yet they who are so frequently accused of impatience are wise enough to realize that the only way you can achieve something absolutely different from what has gone before is to admit that you are working toward something which in its details exceeds your present possibilities of formulation or even of comprehension— while at the same time you steadily move toward a position from which you can see the new begin to emerge. The traditionalists judge specific measures by whether or not they fit in smoothly with known and treasured values. The heretics estimate in terms of the degree to which the actions in question serve to support and clarify the emergent values.

The most serious charge is that of violence and intolerance. Most of us are dissatisfied with the claim that revolutionary violence is a justified response to the violence of established repression and that the refusal to tolerate intolerance is defensible as a means of serving the ultimate aim of freedom. We recognize that there is truth in both parts of the argument; yet inevitably we realize that this is exactly the line of thought which has been used to justify history's long list of crimes committed at the bidding of a scrupulous conscience and revolutions which destroyed thousands of lives only to set up new forms of repression. I suppose that up to a point we have to recognize that, when it comes to justifying force and revolution, there is no theoretical criterion which can be applied with certainty to solve particular conflicts. If one honestly believes that by inaction he condones and supports the evil of a greater violence than any violence on his own part would commit, then his conscience will compel him to resort to force. This is the justification which the Allies invoked in their attack upon Nazi Germany; it is the logic behind the Law's recognition that killing in self-defence is not homicide; it is the reason for the maintenance of a domestic police force and for the proposal by world government advocates that there should ultimately be an international police force to prevent future wars between nations. If by violence we mean the bodily injury of another person, we may recall that on almost every occasion of student riots, it was the police who first decided the point at which recourse to violence to prevent violence was called for.

I am not willing myself to condone the deliberate employment of bombs or arson or any device which is calculated to inflict physical harm on human beings. Nor can I approve of the destruction of computers and libraries, acts of vandalism pathetically reminiscent of episodes in the early days of the Labour Movement when workers attempted to wreck the machines which were both the symbol of their servitude and their only means of livelihood. To plan for an armed conflict in which human lives are counted in advance as expendable would be particularly indefensible procedure for a group which has consistently condemned war as such. For most people, however, this is not the violence in question. What is at issue is the time-honoured weapons of strikes and civil disobedience, the obstinate refusal. What really divides traditionalists and heretics at this point is not the question of whether the methods are justifiable. It is the way in which they view the present crisis.

Obviously the split between traditionalists and radicals is no Manichaean division between the forces of Good and Evil. Both propose values worth defending; each offers particular dangers which are often inseparable from an ideal which is itself wholly positive. Thus, on the side of the traditionalists, despite the public commitment to the democratic ideal of mass education, there has always been the danger of intellectual elitism, the neglect of minorities, conformity to a single cultural ideal. With the radicals, although their avowed allegiance is the liberation of all men and women, one senses the threat of a reduction to a least common denominator, a new version of herd morality in the global village. If the ivory-tower scholar shows too little concern for the needs of the majority of his fellow men, it seems that in the proposals for the new society, there is no concern whatsoever for the scholar. In the University as it is now, there is at least some reason to fear that thought may become the prisoner of the scientific method, that the technological society which it feeds may, instead of freeing man from Nature, either destroy him as a species or lead him toward a subhuman existence of the sort anticipated in Huxley's *Brave New World*. But if rationality here tends to become dehumanized, abstract, 'thinned out' as it were, there is danger that it may become muffled, distorted, and submerged in the reaffirmation of the validity of non-rational experience. We must remember that lucidity is as valuable as intensity for one who wishes to experience the full range of conscious life. The traditionalists' commitment to the verbal and particularly to the written forms of communication may indeed threaten to stifle new forms of creativity. The study of literature has too often become the study of the history of literature rather than the experience of literature; it has on occasion even become the study of the criticism of the history of literature. Yet one may fear lest the aesthetic dimension be lost entirely in the merely sensual if art is limited to the immediate sensations of incoherent and transient experience as in some of our most recent theatre. There is some justice in the accusation that our process of education is concerned primarily with the achievements of the past. The limitation of our intellectual and aesthetic appreciation to contemporary works would be an even greater impoverishment of human experience.

Finally I conclude regretfully that neither the traditionalists nor the radicals honestly care about the freedom and happiness of the individuals who are educated to live in their societies. The traditionalists are willing to blame everything but the goals and methods of our established educational system for the increasing amount of insanity and violence and lack of purpose in the lives of young and old alike. Having defined the good life as they see it, they consider that their responsibility is solely to ensure that the well-trodden paths be kept open. They are unwilling to restructure the system for the sake of those who declare that they have not found life satisfying within it. Yet I cannot see that up until now the radicals have envisioned for us a society in which all individuals are going to be any more free to create for themselves the sort of existence which they find significant and right for them. They appear rather to have drawn up a picture of a society which is more truly egalitarian. This much is greatly to their credit so long as the equality is not based on new pressures to reduce everyone to the same mould. In radical circles it is customary to sneer at the liberal's belief in the freedom of the individual as amounting to little more than the privilege to compete in a contest where the odds are unequal. Yet if the freedom of the individual is to be redefined as the privilege of living in a society where everyone

H

agrees as to what is the common good of the whole, I think that this is still far from being an adequate ideal.

I am not one of those who think that violent revolution is inevitable or even probable, for the simple reason that I am not so pessimistic as to believe that the general public will permit the degree of repressive violence which is necessary to produce revolution. I am sure that student activism will continue though I am unable to envision what form it will take. In a most important sense, I feel that the protesting students have already won. They have challenged what has been taken for granted. To be compelled to defend a way of life or a set of values or a philosophy of education is to throw it into question. Up until now the activists have obviously not succeeded in effecting a significant reconstruction of either education or society. But they have forced many of us, both as individuals and as groups, to consider how to remedy the evils which we find that we can no longer either defend or overlook and to ask ourselves whether there might not be better ways of accomplishing our professed goals. Most significant of all, we have begun to see that even some of the sacred ends ought not to be considered inviolate. Such a process once begun can never be stopped entirely. At most we can try to deviate it or to render it as ineffectual as possible.

But why should we? Even if one approves of neither the aims nor the methods of the dissidents, the sheer numbers of them should show us that some sort of improvement is called for. Either our own aims are no longer right, if they ever were, or the methods which we have used to implement them are ineffective. One may take the position that one will work to accomplish a revolution in education which will be as complete and as speedy as society is capable of absorbing without damaging disruption and the sacrifice of the human needs of the living generation. Or one may prefer to think of the task as seeing how to accommodate legitimate demands and to make needed modifications without destroying those things which still seem to stand steadfast as the framework within which human progress is possible. The only position which seems to me both indefensible and impossible to sustain is the view that there can be nothing new under the sun and no need to question what is here already.

IV

BREAKING THROUGH

How to behave in an age of crisis and transition? What sort of conduct is appropriate? A particular individual may have the possibility of choosing whether to involve himself actively in one sector or another or to withdraw from all active engagement and await results. A society does not have this option. Neither does an institution when it has itself become a centre of conflict. For the purpose of this discussion I am excluding from consideration the negative stance of pure defence although undoubtedly this pattern of behaviour will be adopted by many people who, out of various motives, will fight to preserve the standing bastions intact. I believe that this point of view is as mistaken as it is futile; in any case it needs no discussion, for its methods will be as familiar as what it strives to maintain. I should like to assume that the existence of a crisis in education and particularly in the University has been sufficiently demonstrated. My aim is to consider what we can do in a period of conscious transition to realize to the fullest and in the most constructive way possible the obvious fact that education, which has so often been defined as the transmitter of tradition and past knowledge, is potentially the most effective and ultimately the absolutely necessary instrument for profound social change. The initiation of changes within the educational process is clearly the first step.

There are at least three ways by which an institution may set about the task of radically transforming itself in aim and structure and function though one of them at least seems to me to be already blocked off. That would be to assign various committees to study particular problems and then take no action whatsoever until the reports had been thoroughly discussed – at which point – even if we grant the sincerely good intentions – there would have to be other committees to decide how to correlate the results and meet the consequent problems of the first set. The pressures of the present crisis simply will not allow this recourse, and it is easy to understand why those who propose it are suspected of being in bad faith.

A second approach has been proposed by some of the militants, but almost nobody has taken the suggestion seriously. This is to shut down the University for a period of time and reopen it upon a different basis. Put in this way, the idea is so shocking that we may conclude that only a violent revolution would make it possible. A radical friend of mine remarked quite seriously that in the long run we would all profit if for a two-year period the University would suspend all normal activity while everyone within it participated in an intensive programme of Black Studies. I do not think we can rightly dismiss such a proposal as totally unjustifiable and void of merit. If by this means a society could make significant progress in learning how to eradicate the evils of racism, once and for all, the investment of two years of everyone's time would be repaid a hundredfold. But along with its impracticality, the suggestion is hopelessly one-sided. It would be as if a band of firemen should resolve to save the living room of a house while neglecting the flames burning alongside and in the basement. Perhaps equally unlikely but tremendously attractive would be the possibility that for a year or two the University, students, faculty, administration, would devote themselves full time to the study of the problems of the University in today's world. If all were genuinely involved in such an undertaking, I cannot believe that even those whose formal training for careers was interrupted would not gain far more than they would lose. Obviously this will not happen and cannot happen. Pure persuasion would never succeed in producing such an unheard-of disruption in the normal course of affairs; force would distort the results. And perhaps, cynical as the admission may be, we must admit that, if absolutely everyone engaged in such self-study, the sheer weight of united timidity and mediocrity might paralyse the whole endeavour.

The third way is not a single approach or procedure but involves the adoption of certain specific attitudes as well as the proposal of a few definite steps to be taken. One of the first things to be accomplished is to find some means which will force members of a university to recognize that the present crisis demands immediate action and openness to suggestions for basic changes and at the same time convince the militants that purely negative, disruptive demonstrations are no longer necessary. In short, the faculty and administration must listen, and the dissidents must be convinced that they are being heard. Only when both sides are persuaded that their good faith will not be abused, can we hope that delaying tactics and non-negotiable demands might be replaced by dialogue and communal action. A remarkably sensible suggestion for this preliminary and essential step has been made by Harry Edwards, the leader of the Black activists at Cornell.

If you really want to resolve these problems within the democratic process and avoid violence and confrontation, the only thing to do is to call a constituent assembly of the entire university every semester, in which you would discuss what problems the university faces and what steps should be taken to solve them, and then open the whole thing up to suggestions. Give students a chance to take the microphone and make themselves heard. The assembly would prepare reports on what has been done, what the university is trying to do, where the students have failed in following up their own demands and how they can most effectively participate in the decision-making process . . . I don't care if the school stops all business for a week each semester to hold such assemblies, but it's got to be done. This way you'd really be *dealing* with problems, not just cooling off pressure and postponing a worse conflict.[1]

A constituent assembly is a bit more than an assembly of constituents. Under certain circumstances such conventions are empowered to alter constitutions or to draw up new ones. I do not know exactly what Mr Edwards had in mind. It would hardly be practicable for an all-university body to frame and work out the details for its own comprehensive reorganization. I should think, however, that it would not restrict itself to the airing of grievances but would consider more comprehensive changes in the aims and goal of educa-tion and in the structures which have been established to accomplish them. Biannual meetings of this kind would serve more than one purpose. In addition to providing a device whereby all parts of the university community would for once be brought together, it would keep alive the sense of crisis and urgency. It would also compel would-be reformers to work out details for implementing their plans and to formulate their long range goals more clearly. If the mass assemblies were followed up by committees of combined students, faculty, and members of the administration, all of whom knew they would be forced to report a few months later on specific proposals, I think we would have a reasonable combination of efficiency and full participatory democracy.

Constituent assemblies will not achieve anything more than has been accomplished by student governments and spasmodic 'confrontations' unless we can cultivate in the minds of university personnel attitudes which are appropriate to this period of crisis and conscious transition. First and

[1] 'The Playboy Panel: Student Revolt', op. cit., p. 105.

foremost, there must be a willingness to experiment. Here the professor is pivotal. To give credit where it is due, university administrations and even the Government are often more willing to support educational experiments than the faculty are to ask for it. It is hard to tell just why this is true. I do not believe that professors are congenitally or by training more inclined to inertia than other members of the human species. Mostly, I suppose it is because the individual professor or academic department is afraid that radical changes might seem to his colleagues to result in lowering standards and slighting the requirements of his discipline. It is perfectly true that, if you lay stress on one value, another may be slighted. At long-established institutions, there is a particularly heavy weight of tradition and the fear that relaxation of time-honoured expectations might undermine what has been won. One would think that younger institutions might take advantage of their fresh start to search for novel ways of doing things. To some slight degree, I believe that this has happened. Too often anxiety lest their students might not be accepted and approved by already respected academic departments leads professors to imitate scrupulously the model institutions until they have won the right to set their own standards of excellence. Obviously the day of liberation never comes or is never recognized.

Yet willingness to allow if not to participate in experimentation is absolutely essential unless we are to advocate that compulsion and repression be exerted by one side upon the other. Many people find it difficult to distinguish between chaos and forms which are unfamiliar. One can see that the abolition or modification of existing patterns would impair or destroy certain cherished values. To see, even more to *feel* the importance of values to be derived from situations not yet experienced requires more power of imagination than most of us possess. We resist out of prejudice – in its basic sense of pre-judging; at the same time our sense of the relativity of all human judgments fills us with fear. We are sure that our tested world of values is the only one and haunted by the suspicion that other people, if allowed to challenge it, may find it lacking.

Those of us who are not thoroughly convinced that present educational practices are the best to be found will find it easier to allow that something unguaranteed and possibly unwise might at least be tried. Others will argue that in education we are dealing with human beings, not guinea pigs, and have no right to experiment with a whole generation. Although even this argument tends to make the false assumption, that it is always better 'to bear those ills we have', I will acknowledge that there is some validity to the objection that we should not impose upon everyone the one-sided theories of a few, no matter how impeccable their benevolent social intentions. Nor does it seem to me right that the legitimate needs and interests of those whose life is inextricably bound up with traditional patterns should be ruthlessly denied. That is why I cannot wholeheartedly favour what has been going on under Mao in China, despite the fact that for thousands of oppressed peasants and workers there is undoubtedly an improvement in their daily existence and a broadening of their horizon of opportunity. We should seek for methods by which we may correct existing evils immediately and allow for specific innovations in education without thereby either creating new oppressed minorities or blocking the gradual emergence of more comprehensive changes. There is every indication that the twentieth century is moving toward a new kind of cultural synthesis. During the period of transition we ought, insofar as it is possible, to allow the new to develop alongside the old without their mutual detriment. In the area of education, what we need is more denominationalism and more inner diversity.

By denominationalism I refer to differentiation between one campus and another. Theoretically we have always had this in the United States where any group has been free to found a college if it could secure sufficient financial backing. Over the years, as Jencks and Riesman have shown, the repeated pattern has called for the gradual diminution of the original distinctions which, in any case, were usually restricted to such things as religious orientation or discrimination in the selection of students on grounds of sex, race, or church affiliation. So far as educational variation is concerned, there has been a deplorable 'scarcity of models'. This situation has come about partly as the result of accreditation agencies which apply the same impersonal criteria to all institutions. For undergraduate colleges, there is the even stronger pressure of ensuring that their students will be accepted at whatever graduate school they may choose to apply. Since there is little or no variation between one graduate school and another except in their ability to attain a single ideal, teaching has become a profession where the standard for the kind of student to be produced is almost as rigid and as academic as it is for scholarly publications.

Jencks and Riesman have made a wise suggestion in this connection.[1] Recognizing that large universities will usually be the last to adopt far-reaching innovations, the two authors have suggested that the brightest hope for educational diversity from one institution to another may lie within reasonably easy reach of those small colleges which are now in serious financial difficulty and which recruit for their declining enrolments only those students whose financial resources are so meagre or their scholastic achievements so low that they cannot be admitted elsewhere. Jencks and Riesman refer particularly to the less affluent church schools, Negro colleges, and colleges for women. In an age where there is an increasing

[1] Jencks and Riesman, op. cit., especially chapters VII-X.

reluctance on the part of women, Negroes, and, say Methodists, to go to schools set up just for them, it is the very desire of these institutions to provide exactly what is offered by other schools which has undone them. Here is a superb opportunity for a college to develop a new set of educational aims – in curriculum, degree requirements, classroom procedure and independent student research, community involvement, whatever imaginative faculty and administrators can propose. These experimental programmes might, in a few instances, be offered to the same clientele as before; they might far better allow solely their educational commitments to distinguish them, rather than creed, sex or race, and open their doors to all who could meet the qualifications for the type of programme offered. Obviously money would be needed, too; otherwise there would be merely another version of the old mediocrity. Under these new circumstances, the Government could and most certainly ought to provide federal grants for at least the first few years during which the college would be in process of proving the worth of its offerings. It would be absolutely vital, of course, that no governmental agency should dictate the use of the money beyond the normal demands of legality and social equity. Someone may object that in view of today's climate of opinion, certain of these new or newly organized claimants for federal aid might be pledged to a type of education which would result in the undermining of the social structure which supports the Government. Although I should have to admit that we can hardly expect even an enlightened national government to contribute knowingly toward its own subversion, I do not see any excessive danger or difficulty here. A college which is genuinely interested in the total education of students will hardly propose a programme of simple political indoctrination. Even now the right to disagree with national policy is enjoyed by many faculty

recipients of federal grants although there has been a reluctance on the part of some politicians to extend the same
privilege to students. If there should be a tiny minority of
institutions which the Government refused to support, I
would hope that they might secure endowments from
private groups or foundations which, somewhat paradoxically, have been more tolerant of dissent than our Congressmen.

Such denominationalism would help to advance the cause
of educational reform by providing for the incoming student
the opportunity to choose among a wide variety of types of
training rather than simply to search, within his means and
talents, for the best of a single kind. There are, of course,
two obvious difficulties. First, if the experimental colleges
are to offer anything more than variations on a theme, there
will arise the problem of whether the graduate will be fitted
for the job or profession or graduate school which he hopes to
reach after his college course has been completed. Until the
principle of denominationalism was firmly established, I
suspect that the students who chose the unconventional
curricula would be those who were the most courageous or
the most dissatisfied with standard offerings or both. Obviously
they would have to be careful in balancing probable gains and
losses. This is true for the handful of young men and women
who attend the few non-standard colleges which we do have
– St John's, for example, with its neo-classical curriculum
or, at the opposite extreme, Prescott College in Arizona with
its emphasis on man-in-the-natural-environment.

I believe that ultimately there would be far less of a problem
in relating college training to life 'in the world' than there
is now. One of the chief motives for establishing new types
of colleges would surely be the hope of making the students'
work more relevant. Usually the word 'relevant' nowadays
is used in the context of social responsibility. For my part,

I think that there are a number of ways in which the studies which undergraduates pursue ought to be brought closer to life outside the classroom. But 'relevance' may refer also to the future occupation of a man or woman. Students have objected to what they believe to be a concerted effort on the part of society to train them as replacement parts to keep the economic and industrial life of the nation functioning in its accustomed channels. Employers, on the other hand, often complain that what their young employees have learned at school is of no practical value. One obvious way of meeting both objections is for students to study the skills and activities of their prospective profession or vocation in close relation with their social environment, perhaps to be involved in community projects where they may participate in action research or in a twentieth-century equivalent of the old apprenticeship. With regard to those positions where all that is needed or expected by the employer is a general education in the liberal arts, there seems to be every reason for furthering Harry Edwards' ideal of the 'generation of generalists' who train for life and citizenship, as it were, rather than as experts in a given field.

One objection which may be raised against the idea of encouraging radical diversity among educational institutions is that there is danger of our falling into the trap of developing an even sharper cleavage between the intellectual elite who receive a liberal arts education and the less gifted or economically poorer who settle for technical training in glorified trade schools. Waiving the questions of whether training in technology is really inferior to theoretical work in the sciences and humanities, I should agree that we ought to oppose strongly any plan whereby children are effectively selected at an early age for a type of education which at the start and continually thereafter will train them in preparation for a predetermined place in the socio-economic structure.

This is exactly my criticism of the present system, and it is not only the minority groups which suffer. John Keats begins his book, *The Sheepskin Psychosis*, with a preposterous but all too realistic description of the way that parents will vie with each other to get their children into certain nursery schools which are in turn affiliated with elementary and high schools with impressive records for placing their graduates in distinguished colleges and universities.[1] In his discussion Keats is less concerned with the chances of those whose early training is inferior than with the acute unhappiness of the 'successful' whose lives have been prescribed along lines which they have not found suited to their own personal interests and aspirations. What I am suggesting is the very opposite of this sorry state of affairs. I am pleading for horizontal differentiation, not vertical, for diversity in methods as well as subject-matter, for the elimination of the notion that education can be measured in millimetres of excellence by one standard. Rather than starting a person early on one unswerving path, I should like to see the way made smoother for the child or youth or adult who discovers that there is a better choice for him than the one he made earlier.

I do not believe that the difficulty of entrance into graduate schools from colleges of widely varying kinds presents an insurmountable problem. I suppose we should anticipate two stages. At first the person who intends to apply for the kind of professional and scholarly training which the established graduate schools have been offering would find it wise to go to one of the traditionally structured undergraduate colleges. Even here, however, I should hope that he might find one of the new colleges or newly reconstituted colleges which could offer him the opportunity to master traditional disciplines and subject-matter requirements in new ways. If we are able to achieve the climate of opinion on which any hope

[1] John Keats, *The Sheepskin Psychosis*, New York, Dell, 1967.

of improvement is based, then we may expect that, during the transitional period, departments in graduate schools will be willing to modify and adapt their admission requirements so as to accept applicants whose training might be better than average in some respects but who might have specific deficiencies by traditional criteria. Gradually, of course, the principle of denominationalism would be extended to graduate schools, too, which at present are scarcely differentiated at all except in the quality of their libraries and in their ability to attract distinguished professors with long lists of publications.

Another problem arising from the diversification of colleges would be confronted by the student who found himself dissatisfied with the place which he had chosen; such dissatisfaction would be especially likely to occur if institutions were to assume a more strongly individualized character. At present it is relatively easy to transfer so long as one moves among institutions which are equally accredited and which have not severely limited their enrolments. If we are to encourage denominationalism, we must expect all institutions to hunt for solutions to take care of these new problems. Far from discouraging the wish to move from one place to another, I should like to see a plan established whereby students might take advantage of the unique offerings of more than one college, perhaps simultaneously taking courses in two or more colleges or universities in the same geographical area. I can easily imagine someone remarking that this is the ideal of bees sipping clover from one field to another without settling down anywhere. But I should like to remind my fictitious objector that honey, after all, is made and stored by these wandering insects. The desire to share in varied types of educational experience might on occasion be the mark of the dilettante; it might also be the way to implement a carefully conceived plan. Similarly, an abrupt change in preparation for a career is not necessarily an indication that a person cannot be relied on to do well in anything. If a student wanted to make a really radical shift, he might have to do so with the realization that he would pay the price of an extra period of time to be spent before graduation. In extreme cases there might be so many difficulties as to make the proposed change virtually impossible. This would certainly be nothing new. A freshman now enrolled at Jones City Junior College is certainly not going to transfer to Yale University and for far less defensible reasons. It would be important that the person who realized that he had invested considerable time and energy as the result of a seriously mistaken choice should be allowed to begin over again without being penalized. At present the academic verdict on the student who shifts majors in the junior year or the adult who tries to start a new career late in life is that he is irresponsible, not serious, not to be counted on. We have finally established Head Start programmes for boys and girls who would otherwise be unable to compete in the public schools. We still do everything in our power to block the person who wishes to make a *fresh* start at any level.

Just as important as differentiation among programmes is the principle of diversity within a given institution. Here the idea of experimentation may give us that saving grace which we need if we are ever to move from theoretical speculation about academic restructuring to the practical implementation of new ideas. Faculty members who could never be persuaded to vote for a revolutionary innovation to be adopted universally will sometimes consent to let others play around with something really drastic so long as they don't have to participate in it themselves. Occasionally they are even willing to join in a more moderate experiment providing that it is for a limited period and with the guarantee that there will be a chance to evaluate the results and vote on the proposal again. If our transitional period is to be anything more than an evasion or playing for time, we must take care to ensure that freedom from compulsion to experiment does not result in an indefinite prolongation of the *status quo*. I see no reason whatsoever why, given the capacities of a large university, it is necessary for all students to use the same ladder in working toward the same degree. We are already accustomed to the practice of allowing diversity of subject-matter so that a student may choose among widely varying disciplines for his area of concentration. In the United States we often add an arbitrary list of other required courses in order that he may be 'educated in breadth as well as in depth'. A few colleges are relaxing or removing these general requirements and beginning to allow interdisciplinary programmes as well as the old departmental major. Almost none will permit individuals or groups to work outside the traditional pattern of specific courses and credit hours; very few are willing to dispense with mathematical or letter grades. At most a pass/fail arrangement is permitted for a few special classes outside the sacred major – in other words the non-serious courses which a student takes because he is interested in them and not as a part of his real education. As an absolute minimum, we should not only allow but encourage faculty and students to work out together new plans by which students may prove that in ability and achievement they have earned the all-important degree and diploma.

At this point we must distinguish between three kinds of problems. To start with, there are the very specific issues which grow out of the immediate social crisis, which must be faced at once unless we are to risk violent revolution, and for which the solutions may, by the very nature of the problem, be temporary or provisional. An obvious example is the question of what to do with the disadvantaged groups which demand equal educational opportunity for individuals

I

who have for years been denied the means to prepare themselves to take advantage of it. Another is the question of
whether and how to incorporate special courses which are
demanded as the result of our increased awareness that a
social crisis exists. The most obvious example is Black
Studies, but one could just as well mention proposals for
study of war and peace, of the Vietnam War in particular,
the war on poverty, or specific problems in ecology. Unless
the history of the next few decades is one of total regression,
these problems will soon cease to be posed in the foreground
as exceptional cases. Enlightened legislation will either
abolish the conditions which produce the disadvantaged
minorities or will offer special help to children long before
they are ready to apply for admission to college. Although
there may continue to be a few courses in Black literature
or Black history, the better solution would be an awareness
of the presence of the Negro race at all periods in an integrated
study of human culture. The Vietnam War will be a subject
for history rather than of political science. We may hope that
the study of war would be finally relegated to subdivisions
of studies in abnormal psychology or mass insanity. If this is
too much to expect, then perhaps provisions for research in
methods and institutions for maintaining peace should be
made a standard University offering. Ecology will undoubtedly be taken for granted as an important area of human
concern for all time to come, as unquestioned in its importance
as cellular biology or sociology.

Another of today's dilemmas seems at first thought to be
one of those which are peculiarly of the present moment.
This is the question of the governance of the University.
The students' demands for participation do not arise primarily
as the result of the logical and theoretical extension of their
support of the principle of participatory democracy. They
want fundamental changes instituted immediately, and they

are reasonably sure that not much will be done unless they are in a position to force issues. To this extent the demand is comparable to the insistence that a department of Black Studies be established in order to overcome the appalling ignorance on the part of Blacks and Whites alike concerning Black contributions to the history of civilization. Yet in so far as the students want power to suggest the permanent restructuring of education for the future as well as to solve a few specific problems for the present, we are led into entirely different kinds of considerations. This second type of problem is less specific but more far-reaching. It involves the measured transcendence of which I spoke earlier, the attempt to go beyond all which we have taken for granted, toward a new state of society where the educational structure will be radically different because it will be designed to develop new kinds of human beings with different 'life styles'. The first type of problem is quite concrete; preferred solutions will vary, but it is obvious that some steps have to be taken and the alternatives are limited in number. In the second area, the difficulty consists primarily in defining the problem, in stating just what it is that needs to be accomplished as well as to propose appropriate measures for improvement. There will be a certain utopian flavour in some of these discussions, and there ought to be. Finally, we must think about those things which must be done if there is to be any progress anywhere in either of the other kinds of problems. I have already suggested three things which seem to me to be absolutely indispensable: the decision to allow for daring experiment when the results can in no way be guaranteed, the support of widely differentiated institutions of learning, and the provision for greater diversity within a given school at any level.

There is another quite specific measure which, in my opinion, must be taken before we can seriously attempt any reform which is more than tinkering. This is to change the present practice of assigning definite grades for particular courses or credit hours. In a sense everything hinges on this. If the proposal is to admit members of minority groups who don't meet the usual admission requirements, inevitably someone will ask, 'But since their background is deficient, how can they make the grade?' What he means is that these students would probably fail to make passing grades, hence would have to drop out, in which case all the effort on everybody's part will have been a waste of time. Or else the student would have to be given good grades patronizingly as a kind of gift, which would be unfair to the others who really 'earn' them. More and more, grades come to resemble money, and the old adage, 'It takes money to make money', still holds. It is grades which necessitate the giving of final examinations and which restrict their content to what can be fairly measured. Grading is at least partially responsible for our practice of arbitrarily cutting up the student's programme into so many units of work. Grading demands that there be sufficient uniformity in what students do so that there is a common basis for reward of performance in the coin of the realm. Although grade schools may have originally been so called because they reflected a fixed number of steps up which the pupil had to climb, 'graded' school would be a more accurate term. Grades equal judgments, and inevitably they are accompanied by report cards. In Europe at the University level, the grading process is reserved until the final awarding of the apocalyptic master grade at the end of the student's years of study when he takes the final examinations for his degree. But this is no better inasmuch as the questions and criteria are of necessity objective, factual, impersonal, and the student is often judged solely by this one performance without consideration of whatever he may have accomplished or demonstrated concerning himself in the years preceding.

But surely, someone will say, there has to be some sort of formal evaluation! I agree. But evaluation is not the same as grading or even as ranking. The word 'evaluation' may hold a few unfortunate connotations of cash value or of judgment as to what or who is better than which or whom. But value is legitimately and necessarily a key factor in human life. One cannot live without seeking, finding, and choosing values, but the scale is not always and need not be solely vertical. One values things and people for various reasons and in appropriate contexts.

What would happen if all grades were abolished completely? The reaction of many teachers would be to envisage absolute chaos. For the immediate present, university professors would expect that attendance at their lectures would be decimated, students would not hand in assigned papers, all but a tiny fraction would refuse to exercise the self-discipline necessary for mastering any demanding discipline, they would become dilettantes, would do sloppy work, etc., etc. This Calvinist belief in the basic unworthiness of most human creatures cannot really be documented, and it is an indictment of teacher as well as student if the rewards of learning have become wholly identified with the external stimulus of academic rating. There ought to be better carrots at the end of the stick than that! Some of the reported disillusioning experiences when the threat of grades has been removed can be explained by the fact that exceptions have been made within a system left basically untouched. For example, I have found that some of the students who have availed themselves of the opportunity to take a class for pass/fail have quite obviously done so in order to be able to do less than would be necessary if they were working for a grade which they would be willing to have counted in their recorded Grade Point Average. Their motivation, however, was not to avoid work which they regarded as drudgery but to be assured of having the time required for mastering material on which they would be conventionally graded in their major subjects. These students were not in the majority. Moreover there have been many reports of experiments where removal of the grade threat has resulted not only in a more relaxed frame of mind in the student, but in superior performance in the amount and quality of work done and – most significant – in increased willingness on the part of both student and teacher to engage in projects which involved interdisciplinary problems or allowed the student to work more creatively and to do original research in contexts suited to his own experiences and particular qualifications. Man tends to avoid the uncomfortable, but one can argue that activity is a more natural and less painful state than boredom. It must be admitted that not all aspects of academic work are immediately interesting, but the use of grades to make the end seem worth the means is intrinsically artificial. For the cynic who insists that, without the stimulus of social approval and material reward, nobody will exert himself to capacity, we may point out that we have not said that we will provide for no evaluation at all. What alternatives do we have, and how important really are grades in doing what is claimed for them?

For many people the ultimate aim of education is preparation for desirable employment. It is taken for granted that a candidate's educational achievements as reflected in his grades will be a most important factor if not absolutely decisive. I am sure that some employers attempt to hire graduates with high grade point averages, at least to the extent of preferring those who are ranked in the upper half rather than those who have barely squeaked through. I doubt that many distinguish between 3.4 and 3.6, or between 2.4 and 2.6 even though these figures enclose the magic boundaries which separate B from A above and C below. Certainly most persons are more strongly influenced by the letters of recommendation which accompany the transcripts, by the relevance of the student's training and experience to the position under consideration, and by his performance at the time of the interview. John Keats offers evidence to support his cynical statement that many employers deliberately avoid graduates with brilliant records and favour the average or mediocre student who may be counted on to take orders and not want to run things himself.[1] I suppose that in this case the grades are indeed useful to those who are hiring, but it seems that verbal appraisals of the applicant's abilities and personality would serve just as well. So far as predictability of future success in the chosen career is concerned, there is overwhelming evidence that, except for the student who stays within the academic hierarchy, there is no positive correlation whatsoever between a person's academic transcript and success in his later career. The consequences to be drawn from such data have bearing on more than the grading system, but we may safely conclude that for prospective employers, grades are not indispensable. Even in the appointment of new faculty at the university or college level, the grades which the candidate has received are of minor importance in comparison with the written evaluations of his professors, the nature of his dissertation, and his ability to bring in appropriate references to scholarly works and authors – as well as more significant discussions – at the time of the all-important interview.

In the matter of job distribution, there is no reason why such utility as grades do provide could not equally well be taken care of by expanded and more detailed letters of recommendation, accompanied by a three to five page summary drawn up by the student himself, listing the courses he has taken, papers he has written, special projects which he has

[1] John Keats, op. cit., pp. 14-16.

carried out, and whatever he considers pertinent. If anyone is going to insist that the student's own written record cannot be trusted, I suppose we could attach a requirement that the paper be approved as truthful by a committee of professors who are in a position to judge and that the document be kept in the student's official file at the placement office.

The second great argument for grades is that they are irreplaceable as a means of indicating whether a student is prepared to advance to the next stage of his education. Especially vital is their alleged indispensability for admission into college or graduate school. Imagine a situation in which the admissions personnel of one of our top colleges would have no mathematical evidence by which to judge their hundreds of candidates! To make the situation as difficult as possible, let us further assume that our proposed abolition of grades has not as yet been accompanied by any alterations in curriculum and course structure which would offer possibilities of objective accomplishments not now available. Looking first at the transition from high school to college, it seems to me that the teachers would certainly be capable of sorting out those pupils who could reasonably be expected to do the work required by colleges with high academic standards. Within the group thus selected, admission officials could continue to apply, as they do now, whatever criteria they believe to be effective in selecting particular individuals from among those already deemed superior to most. The truth is that neither high school grades nor the various types of intelligence and scholastic achievement tests can be shown to have any high correlation with the student's academic accomplishment once he has been admitted to college. As early as 1958 George Williams offered a most convincing argument and set of data to demonstrate the unreliability of the criteria applied by most admissions offices. He concluded:

In many years of watching the results of admissions committees' work in a university having rather celebrated 'high standards' of admission by tests, examinations, and high school records, I have reached this conclusion: If all high school graduates applying for admission were asked to write a short paper, and if this paper proved coherent (not merely 'correct'); if all those who wrote coherent papers were interviewed to exclude those who really do not care about going to college, but want to get married, join the army, go to work, or attend a different university; if all were interviewed to exclude those who would labor under a serious financial strain in attending the university; if all those remaining were placed in a large hall, if a handful of peas were cast indiscriminately over the group; and if every person struck by a pea were forthwith admitted to the university, the overall results, measured by success or failure in college courses, would not differ significantly from those obtained by the hard, expensive, and self-sacrificing labors of the admissions committee.[1]

Williams was speaking of admission to undergraduate work. The step from college to graduate school is easier only in so far as the number of applicants is somewhat smaller and the candidate has two sets of grades to present for consideration: those in his major field, in which he now wishes to specialize, and those in the courses which he has taken to satisfy college requirements or, if he is lucky, a few which he took just for fun. Graduate departments concentrate so emphatically on courses in their own discipline that this fact in itself has had the happy result of leading some universities to relax requirements to the extent of allowing pass/fail grades for courses not taken as part of a student's major. The grades in the field of concentration are still judged essential by most faculty. In some places course grades are combined with or subordinated to scores made on the national

[1] George Williams, *Some of My Best Friends Are Professors: A Critical Commentary on Higher Education*, New York and London: Abelard-Schuman, 1958, pp. 162-3.

Graduate Record Examination. Correlations here are not so high as to be very persuasive. In addition, use of this test tends to stress even more the necessity of uniformity in undergraduate education and to put all emphasis on factual information. If the graduate schools were to grow more imaginative in their offerings and to give greater scope to students' creativity, the GRE would become still less reliable an indication than it is at present.

Instead of tests and course grades, we could allow the applicant to present to the graduate school where he applies the personal record and expanded letters of recommendation which I mentioned earlier. Even in a large undergraduate department there ought to be two or three professors able to give a fair appraisal of the work of a student who has done the major part of his work there. If this is not the case, the fact is in itself too shameful to be offered as an excuse. At present many recommendation letters are of slight value inasmuch as they are considered as little more than an extra, friendly service offered to help a student further his career; the recommender is aware that the academic transcript will be taken as the really valid, objective evidence. If a professor knew that his letter was in lieu of a grade, he would have to take care that his recommendation be concrete as well as accurate. He should describe and evaluate particular projects undertaken by the student and perhaps send along copies of written appraisals of papers which the student has turned in during his college career. This procedure would take more thought and care than is demanded by the simple calculation of accumulated grades. It would demand some more time as well though we must remember that the faculty would now have at their disposal all of those hours formerly spent in devising tests of easily measurable knowledge, in correcting them, and in agonizing over borderline cases. For any true teacher, the process of working with and evaluating students who have been encouraged to be creative in a variety of ways will be far preferable to the acknowledged drudgery of reading through a monotonous collection of imperfect reproductions of what he has given in class lectures. I firmly believe that some such system of student appraisal would be more effective than the present system. Undoubtedly mistakes would be made. A few students might be admitted or excluded from graduate schools contrary to their true merit. On the other hand, the inaccuracy and subjectivity of grading has been even better documented than the claim that grades do not measure either native ability or significant knowledge or the ability to apply in new situations what has recently been memorized. On the whole, the fairness of grades is in inverse proportion to the significance of the examination or paper as a testing device.

Discussions of alternatives for the grading system usually come to a dead end when someone points out that anything else will demand more personal contact between faculty members and students than we can possibly provide in the enterprise of mass education to which we have committed ourselves. It is perfectly true that difficulties increase as the ratio of faculty to students grows lower; this is one of the reasons why I favour giving federal aid to small colleges and encouraging the establishment of still more centres for undergraduate training of various types. Yet there are many advantages which only a large university can offer, and I do not believe that they ought to be paid for by adherence to the principle of impersonal and objective measurement. More imaginative use of graduate teaching associates could do much to weaken our dependency on over-large lecture classes. Students might write individual papers or carry out private research projects to demonstrate their mastery and effective use of material presented in what lecture courses they do attend rather than to take specific tests on factual content. These would not necessarily have to be read and criticized by the professor who gave the course, for they would not be a mere rehash of what he had presented. It would not be beyond the realm of possibility – or the pocket of state legislatures – if every student were to be assigned to a particular faculty member who would serve as his academic mentor for the length of the student's residency. No professor should have more than a small number of such students, for he ought to be free to devote a substantial amount of time to them. Graduate students might aid him and would perhaps be of genuine help as a liaison figure between student and mentor. The advisor should not only give advice and counsel but keep himself informed as to the student's academic activities, receive and record such written evaluations of his work as the student would receive from his teachers. After four years of such contacts, there would be at least one responsible source for a unified and documented view of every student's college career. Of course there will be problems here – as with any other system. We would have to decide what to do if the student feels that his mentor has not been giving him the kind of help he has a right to expect. We should need to consider how to avoid letting a single advisor hold too much power in deciding a young person's future. Under no circumstances should student self-determination be weakened as compared with present practice. Possibly we should face the question of whether all professors are capable of handling such an assignment. But my aim is not to pretend that a foolproof procedure can be worked out ahead of time but to insist that we abandon a method which we know to be seriously faulty and set about finding something better.

Once the straitjacket of a uniform grading system has been removed, then if we are willing to encourage and actively support the principle of denominationalism among institutions and to allow both student and faculty to experiment within a given college or university, I think that much can be done. The one undeniable fact about the existing system is that it is obviously not suited for everyone. Persons who have been happy within it tend to argue that there is no reason why it should be. I agree that not everyone can or should go to college, and I deplore the snobbism which insists on a diploma as a mark of social respectability as well as a requirement for jobs where there is actually no relation between the skills demanded and anything which is taught at the University. But while the question of the desirability of higher education for every individual is part of the problem, it is not the main issue. What we must decide right now is how to deal with the demands of those who have decided that education beyond high school is something they want very much indeed – both the ones who, without special provision, would be excluded from it and the others who have been admitted and who have come to believe that what is offered as higher education is sadly lacking.

Those issues which have been most keenly fought, which have resulted in actual violence or in the temporary closing of universities seem to me to be, with very few exceptions, exactly those where the university can best afford to make concessions without destroying itself. Some examples:

There has been a great hue and cry about the 'unreasonable' and sometimes non-negotiable demand by Black students to set up a Black Studies programme for which they themselves would determine the content and faculty. The screams have been particularly piercing when the person proposed to teach in the programme has been one without the usual academic degree. Now it is true that everything about this proposal is highly irregular and that if, on principle, all non-negotiable demands were to be met, regardless of merit, the University might soon be in serious trouble. But it is an abnormal situation which has given rise to the demand. Rather than asking what would happen if all cases were decided in the same way, we ought to consider the unique needs and probable results of the particular measure proposed and judge the individual case on its own merit. Much conflict and frustration could be avoided if people would ask themselves and reply honestly to the question, 'Just how bad would it be if this proposal which I disapprove were to be adopted?' In the example chosen, it is entirely possible that the Black students would set up a programme which would be valuable by any reasonable academic standard. The supposedly unqualified teacher might in reality be an expert scholar in this new field without ever having formally earned a degree in it. If he turns out to be really poor, the students themselves may request that he be replaced. But let us suppose the worst: Let us assume that some or all of the classes in Black Studies are taught badly, that a disproportionate amount of some students' time is spent on them, and that a few actually graduate with a degree which does not represent as high a level of academic achievement as it does for the rest of the graduating seniors. Even then it is possible that those who have shared in the Black Studies will be better educated in terms of their ability to cope with the life which lies ahead of them. And if not, can one seriously argue that the University has been irreparably damaged or that the situation would have been better if the administration had remained adamant even to the extent of closing its doors? It would be entirely different if what the Blacks are asking were not in response to a vicious racism which has existed for centuries; concession would be immoral if the proposal were one which was designed to persecute or to deny the human rights of others. But at worst it is the granting of special privilege to a few in an effort to compensate for an extreme lapse of justice and humanity. Moreover the solution is almost certainly a temporary one unless all the loudly proclaimed resolves of White liberals to eliminate racism are empty mouthings as some Blacks think they are. If that is true, there is indeed no way to avoid revolution and the question of whether and how to establish Black Studies in the University is too minor to worry about.

Much the same sort of thinking applies to the question of relaxing admission standards for racial and ethnic minorities. Every effort should be made to provide assistance for these students so that they can hold their own in traditional courses. Faculty advisors should attempt to suggest academic devices whereby the student may do work of equivalent quality without being subjected to requirements where his deficiencies put him at particular disadvantage. Even with the best of intentions on all sides, there will be casualties. But without underestimating the unhappiness and psychic trauma of those who will have to face the realization that, even when they were given a fresh chance, they could not make it, I can see no reason for not opening the doors for those who can. The price of freedom is always high, but to live well without freedom is not possible *humanly*.

So long as we reside in a nation where there is freedom of dissent and more than one political party, it is unrealistic to hope that the University as such (that is, all universities and colleges as represented by the individuals who compose them) will assume and strongly support a political position which is against the policy of the government in power, especially if that government has been elected by the majority of the population. I see nothing inherently wrong with the idea that individual institutions might issue statements apropos of particular political issues, providing a large majority of their faculty and students were in agreement. There would be little point in statements which represented no stronger unanimity than was known to exist in the population as a whole. Yet this right to neutrality on the part

of the institution does not mean that a university is automatically justified in constituting itself as the defender of national
policy, nor that it should not use all legal means to oppose a
governmental agency if it attempts to interfere with the
civil rights of either students or faculty. Where student
demonstrations fall short of destructive violence, I personally
believe that the University ought to do everything possible
to avoid using physical force or police arrests to end them. If
the protest or strike is against the University itself, there must
be honest negotiation. If the protest is political, I wish that
the University, like the medieval Church, might be persuaded
to assume the age-old practice of providing sanctuary – at
least for so long as no physical injury was offered to persons
or property. Under no circumstances do I see why it is
necessary for the University to inflict its own penalty on
students who are liable to civil prosecution. (Academic
dishonesty is another matter and is comparable rather to
infringement of private contracts.)

One point at which I feel that universities not only would
be justified but are morally obligated to bring to bear such
pressure as they can concerns the question of granting or
continuing federal aid for students who have been involved
in political activism. The use of this kind of financial threat
against a student is one of the most serious examples of thought
repression and a disgrace to a country which calls itself a
democracy. So long as a person continues to demonstrate
that he is fulfilling his obligations *as a student*, I can see no
justification for cutting off the stipend. The argument
sometimes given is that it is ungrateful and unfair of the
recipient to work against those who support him, but one
should remember that the funds of the national treasury
have not been collected solely from the earnings of those
presently holding political office. Neither is it an adequate
rejoinder to say that the radicals themselves are not always

tolerant of dissent. This is too often true, and it may be a legitimate motive for declining to give one's political support to particular radical groups. It does not justify preventing students from completing their education. To want to cut off the dissidents from future possibilities of learning reveals a low degree of trust in the value of the educational process.

The present status of students with regard to participation in University governance is very roughly comparable to that of Negro children in a community with token integration. Everyone pays lip service to the ideal, and there is a general rush to put one or two students on large committees, often without voting privilege, or to set up genuinely integrated committees for purposes where not much is at stake. I will agree that in many matters where the long-range interests and structure of the university are involved, it would be unwise to give a controlling vote to a few students acting as individuals. On the other hand, there is good reason to argue that even in such matters the collective vote of the majority of the student body, or of such large groups of students as were in a position to have a considered opinion on the matter in question, might well be allowed to carry significant weight. The compromise usually suggested by faculty or administration is that students should be consulted and should act in an advisory capacity. Whether this arrangement is anything more than a futile attempt to find a safety device soon becomes apparent. If all except the most innocuous of student suggestions are dismissed as obviously impractical or not worthy of consideration, this is a clear indication that there is no intention of sharing authority. The students, of course, are tested as to their own good faith. If they simply indulge in emotional, non-specific attacks on the system, or if they make radical suggestions and then treat as mere subterfuge all mention of difficulties which must be met if their proposals are implemented, then one may suspect that

K

these students are playing at revolution instead of seriously endeavouring to institute reform. They are in truth neither revolutionists nor evolutionists but only the newest version of rebelling adolescents.

The most delicate area of decision-making in which students have asked to participate is the matter of faculty appointments and recommendations for tenure and promotion. The possibilities of student abuse of such privilege are enough to make some professors declare that they would change their profession before working under such conditions. Their exaggerated fears envision a situation in which teachers would have to curry favour with students, or at least seek deliberately to make themselves popular, and would fear to judge a hostile student's work adversely for fear of reprisal. More soberly they point out that it would be hardly fair or reasonable for the members of a given department to have their colleagues chosen for them by persons whose experience was strictly limited and who would not be the ones to live with the results of their decision. There is some truth in this last argument though I am uneasily aware that it might be interpreted as supporting the accusation that faculty want to run the university first for themselves and only secondarily for the students. In this as in all other questions concerning student participation, there can be a desirable alternative between a system which would put teachers in a position like that of salesmen or paid entertainers, whose jobs depend on their pleasing their clientele and the practice of treating students as children expected to be wholly obedient to authorities who will decide what is best for their charges.

Harold Taylor has made some wise remarks in this connection. Speaking of faculty and students both, he states bluntly that unless they 'are made responsible for deciding on the rules according to which they guarantee to govern themselves, they cannot be asked to have anything to do with the governing'. The doctrine that the University holds the position of *in loco parentis* has almost vanished everywhere but at a few small and unusually sheltered private colleges, but Taylor's point certainly should apply to all regulations affecting behaviour and structured relationships within the academic community. Taylor holds that preliminary agreements could ease the situation even during the present period of turmoil:

> What is needed is a clear policy which holds students accountable for their actions while giving them equality of power in making the policies which affect them. Coupled with this must be the machinery for settling questions of accountability and behaviour in the university community. Once the policy is set . . . [it] must be applied in such a way that when it becomes necessary to protect the rights of the community against violence by calling for police action, it is a matter of agreed-upon principle and policy, not of *ad hoc* administrative action.[1]

If we assume the possibility of a less tumultuous period of transition, it is obvious that students, who have initiated the demand for changes in our concept of education, should play a major role in discussions involving the reappraisal of standard procedures and the installation of new ones. The more evidence they have that their advisory role is taken seriously, the less necessity there will be to insist on controlling votes or veto power. But I think there is no reasonable excuse for denying to the students a measure of real power both in deciding the future of the university and in continuing to share in its administration. The proposal to put all authority into the hands of the transient student population is no more defensible than to entrust it all to the alumni. Yet, as a minimum, there ought to be some provision whereby student vote would have sufficient weight to

[1] Harold Taylor, *Students without Teachers: The Crisis in the University*, New York and London: McGraw-Hill, 1969, p. 111.

determine decisions where faculty and other university officials are divided. Even in the matter of professorial appointments, student opinion should be given genuine consideration. Under exceptional circumstances it might be possible to make arrangements for the appointment of a 'professor at large' if a person who did not fit the requirements of a specific department had demonstrated his ability to make valuable contributions to the students' educational experiences.

At this crisis in the world's history, our only means of salvation is what Taylor has described as 'the collective will to act humanely'. One cannot dynamite this into existence nor legislate it either. Yet I think it exists in sufficient strength on university campuses to justify the hope that students and faculty and administrators may learn to work constructively together in a common effort to solve problems which nobody can any longer fail to see. At this time of breaking through, we should act at once to fulfil the needs of simple justice without worrying too much as to whether what we do is in harmony with tradition or whether it may result in producing other problems in the future. This will set our consciences free so that we may experiment for the sake of enabling the University to become an instrument for social change and the liberation of man in ways not yet realized. As stepping stones toward our own self-transcendence, we may choose goals which are perceptible and desirable even before we are in a position to see any very clear outlines of a future society. For example: Graduate schools should devise methods whereby students may develop and demonstrate creative imagination in thought and actions instead of being trained solely as scholars and technicians. At every level of the educational hierarchy there should be an attempt to break down the limiting structures of uniform requirements and to encourage diversity. The stranglehold of narrowly defined academic departments ought to be loosened and interdisciplinary studies enthusiastically endorsed. We should encourage new kinds of study – new in both form and content. We should recognize that however much the term 'relevance' may have been abused, the concept is not something to sneer at. Any subject is potentially relevant, and it is a disgrace to the teaching profession that students are unable to see the relevance in such a high proportion of the courses offered to them. On the other hand, there is no reason why the study of specific problems in today's world or the discussion of subjective values should not be considered an entirely legitimate and important part of the student's education.

Sartrean existentialism has defined man as a free process, a self-making. Margaret Mead in her last book[1] has stressed the idea that at this stage of the world's history we should accept change as the basic law and condition of man. Perhaps we are rediscovering the truth of the philosophy of the Greek Heraclitus, to whom has been attributed the saying, πάντα ῥεῖ, 'Everything is flowing'. If we like the metaphor of the river, we should recall that, while one cannot forever hold back the water, one can direct the course of its flow.

[1] Margaret Mead, *Culture and Commitment: A study of the Generation Gap*, Garden City, N.Y., The Natural History Press, 1970.

V

SAFEGUARDING THE OPEN FUTURE

WITH their conscious acceptance of the role of authors of human history rather than revealers of God's historical plan, university scientists and scholars have taken over the traditional concern of the clergy and given it a new dimension. In the area of eschatology, we may observe more than the secularization of clerical function. Individual scientists are beginning to acknowledge that they have assumed the responsibilities of God himself in a way that no medieval Pope could have imagined possible. Anthropologist Edmund R. Leach, the Provost of King's College at Cambridge, has expressed this idea in a succinct and forthright statement in an article provocatively entitled, 'We Scientists Have the Right to Play God'.

Human scientists now have it in their power to redesign the face of the earth, and to decide what kind of species shall survive to inherit it. How they actually use this terrible potentiality must depend on moral judgments, not on reason. But who shall decide, and how shall we judge? The answer to these questions seems to me repugnant but quite plain: There can be no source for these moral judgments except the scientist himself.

Leach goes on to argue that since man has taken over God's powers for creation and destruction, he must be willing to accept as well the role of moral arbiter. He concludes, 'Unless we teach those of the next generation that they can afford to be atheists only if they assume the moral responsibilities of God, the prospects for the human race are decidedly bleak'.[1]

Dr Leach has admirably summed up the problem and taken the first step toward proposing a solution. Yet his answer suggests a curious paradox. I think he is right in recognizing that moral judgments depend on something other than and in addition to reason; they involve values, where emotions make the ultimate choice and intellectual concepts play a secondary part. But Leach jumps then to the conclusion that it is the scientists who should make these decisions. Admittedly the scientist will be better qualified than others to judge the probable scientific results of his research. I cannot see that any special qualifications render him superior to the rest of society in his ability to make moral judgments unless in Leach's opinion (the point is certainly debatable), he possesses more of that rationality which Leach has already declared to be irrelevant or at least inadequate. Many people indeed have argued that scientists engaged in a particular research project represent a *parti pris* and are therefore less able to be objective than other persons. Speaking for myself, I should hold that objective reason ought indeed to contribute its own important part to any moral choice, but I am not content to identify it with the scientific method.

Dr Leach's remarks illustrate several facets of the new eschatology. For the first time in history, humanity is both privileged and compelled to realize that it holds the power to determine the possibility, the direction, and the quality of its future existence as a species. Simultaneously we face the appalling realization that we possess no clear notion of what would be the most desirable kind of future for us or any trustworthy criteria by which we might choose wisely between alternatives. We have not given serious thought to

[1] Edmund R. Leach, 'We Scientists Have the Right to Play God', *Saturday Evening Post*, 16 November 1968, p. 16 and p. 20.

the question of who ought to make these decisions which have never been equalled in importance. We have scarcely begun to mark out for special study those areas in which day-by-day choices are already setting the pattern for the development of the future. Most serious of all, there is no general agreement as to what kind of considerations ought to enter into those moral judgments where reason cannot be more than an instrument.

The University must continue to involve itself actively in eschatology, both because its faculty are engaged in research which is in process of predicting the future by prefiguring the form which it will assume, and because the idea of education for the future will henceforth have much greater significance than it has held during the centuries when training for the future referred only to preparation for a profession or to the development of those abilities which would enrich one's life through appreciation of the cultural achievements of the past.

For purposes of discussion, we may distinguish two separate areas of eschatology – the sociological and the biological. On the one side are the problems of human relationships, social structures, everything which will determine the quality of the cultural life of man. In my opinion, the most important task before us here is to forge a new governing concept of individual freedom which is compatible with communal responsibility. On the other side we behold the vertiginous vista of our own evolution as a species, the necessity of decisions which collectively will predefine not only the social situation but the human condition. In their setting this second kind of question is inseparable from the first; indeed the worst possible way to solve the problems of biological research would be to look at them in isolation from all other considerations.

Without attempting to work out any detailed system of

values or ethical directives, I should like to offer a few minimal guiding principles which seem to me appropriate for a socialized democracy. I take it for granted that the principle of change which has been the dominant characteristic of the last century will continue to be our governing reality. Possibly in the farther future, civilization may come to rest temporarily on some distant plateau, but we are still a long way from there. The attempt to provide a pattern for a philosophy based on change and impredictability may be thought to pose a contradiction. We seem to be in the paradoxical position of the sceptic, who by stating that we can know nothing absolutely, undermines his basic premiss. The same sort of difficulty has been encountered by the existentialists. Postulating the absoluteness of individual freedom, they appeared to lay themselves open to the charge of destroying all possibility for an ethics by reducing everything to spontaneous and arbitrary caprice. Yet the very statement that all persons are equally and totally free simultaneously introduces the corollary postulate that each one is responsible for his actions. Even without God, not everything is allowed. In particular it is not permitted to act as if some persons were intrinsically more valuable than others or to institute structures which are based on the assumption that men and women may be treated as objects.[1] Upon the hypothesis that change is the essence of human experience, we must certainly keep openness to further change as one positive criterion against whatever would deny or prevent it.

In planning for the future, we meet with many sets of conflicting demands and opposing principles. Looking at them in the abstract, I think they tend to fall under two general headings. First, there is the problem of how to care

[1] I have attempted to work out an ethics appropriate to humanistic existentialism in my book *An Existentialist Ethics*, New York, Knopf, 1967.

for both the future and the future perfect; second, there is the question of how to define man and his proper relation to the rest of nature.

In speaking of the future and the future perfect, I do not refer simply to the fact that there are an immediate and a farther future although concern that the human race should continue to exist for many centuries is a central theme of all discussions related to atomic research and the entire field of ecology. In keeping with the ideal of measured transcendence which I proposed earlier, I think it is not only necessary that there should be a future but that we should have a sense of the future perfect. We should work toward the accomplishment of ideal goals – even utopian goals, if you like – with the intention that, at the historical moment of their achievement, men and women will be free to launch out toward other ends which we cannot at present imagine and could not appreciate if they were revealed to us. Paradoxically, we want to set up safeguards for humanity's future without making it impossible for later persons of wider vision to work outside what they will perceive to be life-cramping restrictions.

I have often thought that the ultimate tension in man derives from this banal truth: He judges every situation – past, present, and future – from within a private world structured with himself as centre of reference; at the same time he realizes that his present judgment of a future situation may not be the same as that which he will hold within his later personally structured world. As Sartre puts it, I make a rendezvous for myself down there in the future without knowing who I will be when I show up for the appointment. Relativity, like Sartre's *Néant*, gnaws at the heart of each firm resolve and every attempt at absolute judgment. This is the origin of much of the pathos – and perhaps a bit of the grandeur, too – of the human condition. We behold it in its comic aspect when we observe a man enjoying to the fullest a situation which he had previously vowed to 'avoid like the plague'. With more tragic overtones we watch one who lives with solemn intensity the petty joys and sorrows found in the small day-to-day changes of advanced old age or extreme disease. We are pained and shocked to see him, who would have declared earlier that life on this level was no life, now clinging to it and finding an absorbing interest in it as a total world with its peculiar and varied colorations. Yet who is to say whether it is better or truer to stick by the judgment which, on the basis of present strength, condemns in advance and refuses to risk the possibility that it may learn to accept and find value – or at least acceptable compensation – in what it now abhors? Is Hemingway's suicide an example of mistaken cowardice or of the courageous rejection of mental weakness and personal deterioration? Should we laugh at or admire the young hero of Gide's novel, *The Counterfeiters*, who, after a first night of perfect love, put his head in the gas oven in order that he might never learn to accept days of diminished ecstasy? Do we find a better ideal in Tolstoy's Pierre of *War and Peace*, who recognized that the limits of human joy and suffering are quickly reached and found that when he became a prisoner, the pain of the bonds on his wrist and his pleasure at their removal or at the unexpected beauty of a sunset equalled in intensity all of the sorrows and ecstasies of life in the pre-war world of freedom and luxury?

The individual consciousness structures whatever situation it encounters and lives it one way rather than another as it chooses. Yet we cannot cancel out the surrounding situation. A man may win a psychological victory in a concentration camp or in the torture chamber, and this triumph of the human spirit should never be underestimated. Nobody would seriously argue that the brief exaltation of transcending the restricted situation is sufficient by itself either to justify the society which established the camp and condoned the torture or to persuade the prisoner that his situation is acceptable. One of the worst devices in bad faith which has been exploited by oppressors is to point to the evidence of man's ability to transform and restructure even the poorest of conditions by making them into projects for personal fulfilment and confuse this achievement with true self-realization. It is easy for us to see in the intrigues of the harem or in the house-servant's combination of loyalty to the master and harassment of inferiors a pathetic example of self-imposed degradation on the part of the oppressed; we grasp even more quickly the lie inherent in the attempted self-justification of the oppressor who claims that the victims 'are happy and content as they are'.[1]

Unless we subscribe to the dubious notion that there neither is nor can be anything really new under the sun, we should be prepared to allow for the emergence of attitudes and values which at the moment we would either deny or fail to comprehend. Yet along with this postulation of a future so open that we seek to safeguard the possibility of our later advance in a direction which we would not choose at present, I think we feel the need for some sort of limits. Otherwise we should find ourselves defenceless before the argument that a society like that depicted in Huxley's *Brave New World* offers a fair approach to a realizable Utopia. Except for a tiny minority of disaffected, the members of that society enthusiastically endorsed it and were supremely content. It is from our external point of view that we reproach them for their willingness to support a class structure of masters and slaves, a society where animal contentment was

[1] Simone de Beauvoir discusses this subject in *The Ethics of Ambiguity*, translated by Bernard Frechtman, New York, Philosophical Library, 1948.

the easily achieved ideal of all and where the privilege of dissent was either biologically blocked or psychologically inconceivable. Along with whatever prejudice we may have against physical and material well-being as the final criterion of the good life, we may condemn Huxley's imaginary society on at least two grounds: First, the uncomplaining acceptance of their lot has been secured by dint of removing from them any possibility of their perceiving that a more rewarding kind of existence and a broader horizon of awareness might have been open to them. Huxley's biological manipulation of genes represents an extension of the doctrine that the underprivileged are happier if they are kept in ignorance of the fact that they have not been allowed to choose their fate and that things might have been or could yet be different. As such it represents the ultimate post of conservative politics – the faith that a stratified society and the unequal distribution of wealth are the natural outcome of innate differences in talents and virtues. Whereas the first objection refers to the denial of freedom to the workers, the second is that the upper class has effectively renounced the responsibility of freedom; it has closed the door to all future transcendence. To put it another way, all time has been recast as present. Even if we allow that for the individual there is that natural succession of tomorrows which bring in maturity and eventual decline, there is no social sense of moving toward anything more than eternal repetition. Noticeably lacking is any concept of a future perfect, of a point when a particular motion forward would be completed and give rise to the start of another kind of future beyond the horizon.

Although the context and motivations are entirely different, this is, I believe, the weakness and temptation of radical thought. Sartre has pointed out that at the moment of revolutionary action, there emerges the group-in-fusion, which is united by work done in common to accomplish a desired end against the opposition of the oppressors. After the victory, the enemy becomes anyone who would attempt to destroy this unity; that is, potentially members of the group itself.[1] Thus the original revolutionary group is gradually institutionalized and the individual subjected to the interests of the whole. I suspect it is because they have acted in the name of an ideal absolute – absolute justice, equality, etc. – that the revolutionist finds it hard to envision the possibility that dissent might be other than a disguised form of the old opposition.

I claim that I am justified in directing these two criticisms against the Brave New World in spite of the inhabitants' willing acceptance of it and not simply because it happens not to appeal to me. My own reaction is admittedly based on two assumptions which possibly not everyone will accept: that each human being is by nature free and that the opportunity to develop his own potentialities, freely and creatively, to the maximum degree consistent with the right of other freedoms remains a proper goal for any attempt to improve the social structure.

Whatever our personal philosophical orientation may be, I believe that almost every thinking person today would condemn Huxley's negative Utopia. It is so clearly an example of the cynical and exploitative perversion of human possibilities that it may almost serve as a test case for the adequacy of whatever criteria we may wish to set up. Occasionally problems in real life are equally clear-cut. It does not require much use of the imagination to see that the racism of contemporary society is as indefensible as the creation of sub-human species in the Brave New World. The only legitimate debate will centre around what are the most effective and humane procedures to end it as quickly as possible. Racism

[1] Jean-Paul Sartre, *Critique de la raison dialectique*, Paris, Gallimard, 1960. This is the basic theme of Book II, 'Du Group à l'histoire'.

today is not really a problem but a source of pure conflict of interests in which only the short-sighted are on the side of the defenders.

Most questions concerning the future are more subtle and far less easy to define. One of the most interesting stems from phenomena observed in the present 'generation gap'. What are we to make of the new forms of communal patterns which have emerged within the last decade or so? There is the voluntary crowding together of masses of people for an extended period to listen to music amplified far beyond the point which older persons find endurable, no longer directed towards simple hearing but aimed apparently at the absolute saturation of the senses. There is also the adoption of new types of communes with adults of both sexes and children living under one roof or in closely connected dwellings, in groups totally at odds with the traditional family units. At this point I am not concerned to argue for or against the sanctity of the family as the *sine qua non* of human society. I am interested rather in the phenomenon of what appears to be an acceptance of crowding together as a positive thing and a denial of the values of privacy and independence. Someone once suggested to me that perhaps we are witnessing here the first signs of adaptive behaviour in reaction to overpopulation. Possibly young people who have been raised in over-large families, crammed together in overcrowded schools, accustomed to traffic snarls, jammed beaches, and queues everywhere from the local theatre to registration halls at the university have never developed the taste for being alone. I am not totally convinced that this explanation is true; certainly it is not the only factor involved. One thing, however, is clear; there is a conflict of values, and the resolution of it will have a profound effect on the way in which we view the problems of ecology and population control. If we conclude that guaranteed privacy, the right to live in as small and individual a unit as one pleases, and the privilege of enjoying undisturbed tracts of natural wilderness are inseparable from the good life and possibilities for human development, we will do all within our power and the restraints imposed by our conscience to limit the population and to impose restrictions on production so as to perpetuate these conditions for a population of predetermined size. If we attach greater value to the rights of still greater masses to be born, we shall encourage whatever adaptive behaviour we see developing and insist only that all political and scientific effort be devoted to supporting the sheer existence of increasing multitudes.

In deciding for the future, there is never any simple solution to the task of protecting those values which we believe to be ultimate and enduring while providing also a guarantee of free access for the emergence of new and broader points of view. There is no perfect, unchallengeable solution. Yet I believe we will be on the right path if we recognize that we must always maintain a dynamic tension between certain conflicting and equally fundamental human demands which seem to me to be inseparable from human existence.

First, there is the tension between the need for diversity in opportunity and in ways of individual self-realization and the ideal of equality in opportunity and in the exercise of citizenship. Diversity and equality are not truly opposites. Each in itself is a good, not an excess to be shunned as in the old Aristotelian pair of opposites. Exclusive concern with either will totally destroy the other and end up by being self-defeating as well. Diversity, without the ideal of equality, ends in elitism and injustice. Equality, without provision for diversity, renders meaningless the opportunity it purports to offer. I have argued that the present educational system has – in the name of equality – stifled originality and individualism and at the same time excluded many potential students from any form of higher education. In a socialized democracy, education ought to offer a wide variety of possibilities while making every effort to see to it that each person has full opportunity to choose his own path.

Another aspect of this fundamental tension comes out in the conflict between pluralism and social unity. Unless we provide structures to implement a new 'collective will to act humanely', there is grave danger that independent communities would become new centres of oppression. Yet the concept of 'power to the people' ought to include some measure of self-determination for groups smaller than the nation. Otherwise we simply perpetuate the evils of big, centralized government where representatives have lost contact with their constituents and the general public has no audible voice in formulating the laws which govern it. Certainly the spokesmen for minority groups have no wish to have imposed upon them a uniform cultural pattern, not even if the intentions behind it are wholly benevolent. I think that for the future we ought to work out some plan by which we could, within the larger framework of a state inspired by socialist principles, not only tolerate but actively encourage the existence of disparate communities composed of people who wished to work out a style of life at variance with prevailing patterns. Of course this would create problems. If allowed to become too large, too wealthy and too much separated from the national government, these units could develop into a new set of squabbling feudal mini-states. But in this age of easy communication and travel, I think such a fear is highly unrealistic. More obvious are such questions as the responsibility of the outside community to provide aid in case of emergencies. Would crop failure or an epidemic of hepatitis be considered on the same basis as the tornadoes and earthquakes and floods which already bring in active help from federal sources? And what of the children in such communities? Can their schooling be left wholly at the discretion of their parents? Will they constitute a new group of underprivileged if the time comes when they wish to leave the small community and attend a university in another area? I do not believe that these problems are insoluble, and I think that we ought to be willing to meet them. What I do hold to be intolerable is any society which is so sure of its present attainment of the highest level for all mankind that it can tolerate no differentiation among its citizens.[1]

Transcendence and commitment are inextricable, yet as principles they may clash. In a sense they are simply two aspects of freedom. Freedom *is* the possibility, the impulse to go beyond the existing situation in a new direction. Its actualization demands action and concrete structures in the world. Obviously freedoms frequently conflict. Where individuals are concerned, we may find devices for reconciliation and compromise. It is more difficult for institutions and states to guarantee the right to initiate action to modify their structures while at the same time protecting principles upon which they are founded. It has been demonstrated that insistence on the necessity of restricting protest to established patterns and channels may be a powerful weapon for continuing repression. The plea that the abstract principle of tolerance for all spoken or written dissent is an adequate protection for oppressed minorities is hardly defensible. At the same time I believe that the radical Left is mistaken in

[1] The idea of separate, more or less independent communities is not entirely strange in the United States. There have been a few short-lived utopian ventures. In addition, we may say that the practice has been at least foreshadowed by certain religious groups, for example the Amish in Pennsylvania and Ohio and the Mormons in Utah. The racial doctrine of the latter has recently come into conflict with the federal position on racial equality. It is my view that such groups cannot be permitted to go contrary to the basic provisions for legal and social justice on which their own well-being depends.

feeling that it can adopt easily and unquestioningly the claim that tolerance of all points of view is disguised intolerance. The freedom to express dissent cannot legitimately be denied by any party which claims to favour the liberation of man. If dissent assumes the form of violence, it cannot be defended from within the system but only as revolution. The justification for revolution is always the same, but it is the hardest of all evidence to be identified with certainty and it is very rarely found. It can be only the conviction that the violence done to human beings in the existing state of society is greater than the violence which would be done to those who are to be sacrificed in the process of forcing a change; it must be accompanied by the assurance that no other method can be effective. In my opinion we have not quite reached this critical point and need not do so if we are alert to the danger that we might reach it and to other alternatives.

Let us consider now the other division of eschatology – the attempt to define the human and to prescribe our future as a species in relation to the rest of the universe.

Any attempt to define man must begin by situating him with respect to the rest of nature. The sentimental view of Rousseau and certain other Romanticists – that man is a creature of natural goodness and the best life is a life 'according to nature' – received a considerable jolt in the nineteenth century, partly as the result of the theories of Darwin and other early evolutionists and partly because of the findings of psychoanalysis initiated by Freud. The philosopher John Stuart Mill attacked the position in his treatise, *The Idea of God in Nature*, with the intent of widening the gap between the human and the natural. Mill argued that humanity's greatest material advancements and highest moral achievements have been due to man's ability to dominate over natural forces and his ethical superiority to nature's blind processes. At present there is great interest in the question of man's relation with nature and considerable disagreement. In the light of our increased awareness of the dangers which have resulted from our reckless destruction of the natural environment and our disregard of the consequences of upsetting the balance of nature, there is much talk of the necessity of our respecting nature, of living with it rather than against it, of taking thought for the survival of the planet earth itself as well as for the human species. So long as these problems are seen as purely ecological, debate centres primarily around methods to be adopted and the degree of urgency in the immediate situation. No cause has ever before so successfully crossed party lines and united young and old alike as our sudden realization that we must act quickly if we hope to breathe pure air and drink clean water much longer – or at all. When it comes to philosophical views of man in relation to nature, there is very little unanimity.

Herbert Marcuse, somewhat in the spirit of Mill, lashes out at those who use an appeal to Nature as an excuse for human repression.

Glorification of the natural is part of the ideology which protects an unnatural society in its struggle against liberation. The defamation of birth control is a striking example. In some backward areas of the world, it is also 'natural' that black races are inferior to white, and that the dogs get the hindmost, and that business must be. It is also natural that big fish eat little fish – though it may not seem natural to the little fish.

Marcuse goes even farther than Mill when he states flatly that 'History is the negation of Nature', but the accompanying attractive explanation does not represent man as a ruthless destroyer. Man's mastery is not repressive but liberating. 'Civilization produces the means for freeing Nature from its own brutality, its own insufficiency, its own blindness, by virtue of the cognitive and transforming power of Reason'.[1] Marcuse thinks of man as humanizing Nature. I am reminded here of Sartre's statement that as man carves out his being in the world, as he acts in the midst of things and structures external to him, he makes himself a thing to exactly the same degree as by his action, he constitutes a thing as human. There occurs a kind of 'transubstantiation' (Sartre's word) of human and non-human in every interaction which man has with things.[2]

There is nothing in the positions of Marcuse and Sartre which is prejudicial to the plea that we must be acutely aware of the consequences of our manipulation of the natural world. Ecological responsibility is as important a part of the liberation of both man and nature as the techniques of agriculture, engineering, or biology. Both philosophers, however, frankly adopt the point of view that man and his needs remain central. He is still 'master' of the world. Sartre in particular has never abandoned the position he took almost thirty years ago in *The Flies*, when he declared that man's freedom has made him an exile. Even as he dwells in the midst of nature, man has no natural place.

This view is quite offensive to some of today's radicals. They oppose the idea that man is in any way properly the exploiter of nature and claim that he should look on himself as being a part of nature or, better yet, as a partner with nature. If one presses to see just what this means, one encounters considerable ambiguity. If we take the statement as meaning that our biology links us so inextricably with the rest of the universe, organic and inorganic, that we cannot

[1] Herbert Marcuse, *One Dimensional Man. Studies in the Ideology of Advanced Industrial Society*, London, Routledge and Kegan Paul, 1964, pp. 236-8.
[2] Jean-Paul Sartre, op. cit., p. 246.

alter it without being altered by it and that the network of the natural world is so closely meshed that our existence depends upon our maintaining ourselves in proper balance with it, then I go along wholeheartedly with this rediscovery of an old truth at a time of crisis. If the accompanying attitude bears a closer resemblance to an old form of romanticism, attaching a high value to the psychic nourishment that humans have always found in close association with the life of other organisms and the splendours of the landscape, then it stands as a valuable corrective to our almost lost ability to find joy in the simple fact of existing in a world which can be made to sustain our life and which offers us gratuitous beauties. But if the plea to live in close partnership with nature implies the adoption of an anti-rational neo-primitivism as it does in some circles, then I, for one, view it with suspicion and alarm. I should argue vehemently for the right of the individual or of small groups to work out their own contemporary version of the life of the ancient tillers of the soil or whatever primitive idyll they wish. To advocate a return to tribalism or the cottage industry as a solution for the problems of the world as a whole involves at best illogical absurdity and a lack of realistic thought; at worst it is seriously regressive.

It would be needlessly insulting to the sincerity of young idealists to dwell long on such arguments as the unavailability of sufficient land if everyone should seek to return to the soil or for the need of an up-to-date industrial economy if the offspring of the neo-primitives are not to die of the diseases which made infant mortality so successful a means of population control in the past – not to mention the necessity of electricity for amplifiers at rock festivals. Their plea for simplicity is genuine. Their search for new and more satisfying forms of communal life does not necessarily constitute a menace against the well-being of the conventional majority unless the latter's own insecurities and fears make it into a psychological threat. Provision for the existence of separate communities for dissidents who wish to live apart from society may be the best way of simultaneously meeting the needs of one kind of extremist and at the same time protecting the majority from a hostility which would otherwise be manifested destructively within society. By definition it is not a solution for the social structure as a whole. Moreover the myth of a golden age of happiness before the ravages of what we call civilization is a poet's dream; it is neither historical fact nor a valid sociological hypothesis. Even if such an age of innocence could be shown to have existed once, we cannot return to the Garden of Eden now. We have eaten too generously of its psychedelic fruit, and our expanded view of the landscape is irremediably altered.

The argument that we need to change our concept of man – both of his own nature and his relation to the natural environment – should not be dismissed as being nothing but a sentimental wish to escape from a life which has grown too complex. In a world where insanity seems to be the rule in international relations, where violence, mental aberrations, and retreat into the private world of psychosis or narcotics are frighteningly on the increase, we may note that not only the social dropouts but such important psychologists as R. D. Laing and Erich Fromm suggest that perhaps it is society itself and not the deviants which is mentally ill. To ignore this possibility is to plunge us more deeply into madness. One of the most frequently offered explanations for today's unrest and turmoil is the statement that we have experienced simply too much of rapid change within the span of a generation, more than we have been able to absorb psychologically or sociologically without temporary damage to the personal and political systems. In short, the problem is seen as one of adjustment, comparable to that of the physiological organism which has received a traumatic shock. This view is neither regressive nor defeatist. Its proponents cheerfully set about seeking to relieve the suffering, to cure the symptoms; they assure us that with time and patience things will settle down and get better. What is never brought into question is the overall rightness of the framework within which humanity pursues its adventure. It assumes that the forward movement of human progress has been established and that more of the same is desirable. It is up to individuals to make adjustment. What frightens me about this attitude is not so much its blindness and underlying policy of *laissez-faire* today as the thought of the possible developments to which it might give rise in the future. At present people are given or buy for themselves tranquillizers to help them endure what they do not know how to change. This kind of thinking could lead logically to the practice of treating people from their earliest years with drugs which would inhibit them from feeling the need to protest against a way of life which is taken for granted as desirable. I have heard a scientific colleague of mine argue earnestly that if research should discover that criminals tended to have more of certain chemical substances in their blood than the average presumably law-abiding citizen, then it would be our moral duty to the individual as well as to society at large to guarantee – by pre-natal genetic coding if possible – that his chemical make-up did not include the dangerous substance. Once we take our stand on the principle that the system is right, there is no limit to what we can persuade ourselves to do with the deviant. All of this is offered in the name of reason without seriously questioning whether what passes for the rational ideal is truly reason or not; 'progress' is identified with scientific or technological progress.

It seems to me entirely right that critics of contemporary life should urge that we call a halt and do some profound thinking about the nature of man and the direction in which he is going. It is appropriate that we should bring up the rational ideal itself for questioning and test its adequacy. On the other hand, I do not derive much comfort or encouragement from those who have most loudly challenged the validity of reason and its trustworthiness as a guide for human life. Timothy Leary urges us to exploit the properties of the mind-expanding drugs so that man may speedily achieve spiritual well-being and learn to look on all but the bare essentials of material life as so much impedimenta. The individual is to discover new forms of consciousness and supposedly his access to cosmic consciousness. Personal and social problems are not so much solved as dissolved. 'Turn on, drop out, play Russian roulette with your brain', Leary is reported as having advised an audience of university students. Alan Watts suggests seriously that perhaps the hyper-development of the individual consciousness is an evolutionary dead-end. To pursue it further may result in the extinction or at best the arrested development and eventual atrophy of the human species. In addition to a number of philosophical objections which we might oppose to the proposal that we solve the contemporary problems of the West by a new version of a philosophy which has not proved to be satisfying to the majority of the population in the East, I think that the attempt to cope with the present social crisis by offering an esoteric form of individual salvation is doomed from the start.

In attempting to decide what man's relation to nature ought to be, we meet once again tensions between claims which are equally valid and basically inextricable and yet to some degree in conflict. Most basic, I suppose, is the question whether human fulfilment ought to refer to the historical achievement of the human species or to the experiences and self-realization of each human life. We may express the same idea in a number of other ways. We may look at it in terms of rational understanding as contrasted with personal happiness, or as reason versus feeling, or as impersonal objectivity as opposed to love. On the other hand, there is the old tradition that the highest end of man is to fulfil his thirst for knowledge. This urge is manifested in the thrust toward more and more scientific achievement and the exploration of hitherto unknown territories of the universe. On the other hand, there is the assertion that all of this is meaningless if man's knowledge does not succeed in dispelling suffering for all mankind and bringing him happiness and in teaching humanity as a whole the value of love. Whatever one may feel about the wisdom of the United States' space programme, the public debate held a significance deeper than the question of particular national priorities. It asked in effect whether man should live *for* the future or *in* the present. Those who maintain that the existence of a question requires that we answer it, that the possibility of solving a scientific problem demands that we engage in research to master it are accused of being willing to risk the future existence of man. Those who say that the well-being of every human being now is more important than space exploration and biological investigations are reproached with being willing to settle for simple contentment and human stagnation.

Love is the value offered as the bridge between the individual and society or, if you prefer, as the cement which can hold people so closely together that whatever is conceived as good for the whole will automatically include the legitimate needs of the individual. In spite of my initial impatience with the naïveté which could believe that the ideal of brotherly love is anything new in the world or that it could suddenly now be actualized as a powerful force after two thousand years of formulaic lip service, I have come to believe that it can and should be recognized as a meaningful claim in any discussion of social or political processes or in plans for restructuring. The word 'love' is as slippery and protean as 'justice' or 'truth' or 'democracy', but it describes a reality just as these other terms do. Perhaps, too, we may accurately say that it helps to define a problem more than it provides answers. Theoretically love is always a unifying force; actually it serves to illustrate more sharply than anything else the tension between individuals and the collective. This is because love exists and functions powerfully both as a concrete feeling and as an abstract ideal. When it is particularized and most concrete, it very often becomes exclusive and serves as a force for disunity and a breeder of hatred. We have observed this vividly in every revolution, not only during the struggle for liberation but in the measures adopted after the triumph of the revolutionaries. Along with the partiality of love as demonstrated in living, historical situations, we must recognize the peculiar tension which is present in love as an abstract ideal – as the belief in the brotherhood of man or in the essential oneness of humanity or in the irreducible value of every human soul. In so far as love points to and rests upon human solidarity, it has lost all trace of the particular. It is sharply differentiated from active justice, which makes distinctions of merit and deserving. It affirms the principle that, underneath the superficial differentiations of personality and achievement, all persons are equally valuable. More accurately, the question of equality does not properly enter in, for by his simple existence a human being has the right to be considered for himself alone. Paradoxically, love's assertion of human solidarity leads us to an extreme individualism. To love all mankind is either an empty formula and entails the sort of contradiction posed by the Greeks: 'The man who has the whole world as his friend has no friend'. Or else it asserts the absolute value of and validity of the private world of each existing individual and acknowledges that there is no possibility of reducing them all to orders of rank or category. I do not deny that love and justice may exist side by side – in individuals and in society, but in their fundamental claims they are opposites. Justice rests on the assumption that an impersonal standard of objectivity exists and may be applied fairly to all. Love asserts that, in order to give a person his due, we must judge within the world of which he is the centre. From one point of view, love poses the conflict of private worlds and offers no easy solution for resolving it. Yet since it insists that we all do or should recognize the right of each one to lay claim to this irreducible value, it forbids the individual to be concerned solely for himself or for a particular group. Thus love as an abstract ideal serves as a corrective to the partiality of love as a lived, particular passion.

If we look at love as being the tension between the needs of the person and the requirements of solidarity rather than a mysterious force which would somehow melt all into one, then I think that it becomes the indispensable companion of rationality; both must be present in all constructive thought about the future of man. Love is one of the criteria in our search for a new concept of responsible freedom or of individualism-within-community. Reason and love together may plan for the future of mankind without neglecting the well-being of the particular men, women, and children who will live through the human adventure.

Obviously I cannot presume to draw up a detailed picture of the society which seems to me to meet best the requirements of reason and love and to maintain the most acceptable dynamic tension between the other sets of conflicting demands which I have been discussing. It seems to me just, however, that I should mention a few things in order that my discussion should not remain too much on the level of abstraction or have no direct relevance to the contemporary issue in education.

First of all, I think that without apology or intellectual embarrassment, intellectuals ought to teach, foster, and in every possible way recognize the reality of human solidarity and the requirements which it entails and exerts on each one of us. One may argue that the responsibility of each human being for all others is a commandment derived from God, an obligation inscribed in the very stuff of the universe, the ideal of Love, or the logical result of calculations from pure selfish expediency. It should by now be obvious to everyone that we cannot truthfully or practically continue to equate full humanity with one small segment of the world's population and regard the rest as a subspecies – not on the basis of race or sex or economics or religious belief or cultural achievement or formal education, or innate intelligence. Even if we wished, we can no longer afford to tolerate the existence of oppressed minorities. Moreover it is much too late to attempt to repair injustice by the simple strategy of absorbing the victims willy-nilly into the prevailing cultural pattern of the oppressors. To be a full member of society means to have the right to be accepted as oneself. It should not be thought of as comparable to the position of the child who loses his own name in adoption.

The first requisite is to recognize tangibly that the human race *is* a society. We need to establish a world organization of such a kind that every person effectively realizes his co-citizenship with every other resident of this earth. I am well aware that the possibilities of a repressive government centralized in one world authority makes our present nightmare seem like a modest diversion, but I am not speaking of a tyranny nor of a super-state resembling any which we have known. I do not propose that there should ever be a World

President with powers approaching those of the President of the United States or of the British Prime Minister, certainly not a committee comparable to the Soviet Presidium. We should unalterably reject the notion of a small cabinet to meet in closed sessions. The United Nations does not offer quite the right model either, especially not in so far as controlling members can determine which other nations are to be admitted. Surely it is not beyond the power of human thought and imagination to work out a type of federation which could keep peace, prevent exploitation and repression, and arrange for beneficent world agencies. Most proponents of world government, including the late Bertrand Russell, have felt that, if the organization is to have any effective authority, it must have at its disposal some sort of international police army. The analogy with local and national police does not strike me as a particularly happy one. If military force really is a necessary appurtenance to the power to keep peace and ensure justice, then there must be extreme care to guard against the potential savagery of the watchdogs. There would have to be at least two kinds of safeguards. One set would be designed to guarantee that the world police would never become closely attached to a supreme administration – either to the individuals or to the various offices – in a way which would make it possible for them to rule the world as their subjects. The other would ensure that the police army would never be allowed to grow too large or to possess weapons powerful enough to be used as blackmail. We ought not to think of the purpose of a world government in terms wholly negative; it should do more than control unruly members and arbitrate disputes. As with any benevolent form of government, its function ought to be to provide for the improvement of the life of its citizens. If through mutual co-operation the productivity of all nations could be developed to the maximum appropriate for its size and the number of its inhabitants, and if regions with meagre resources were guaranteed the minimum of whatever necessities would enable its labour to contribute to the world's economy, then I see no reason for those bitter conflicts between nations which have bloodied human history to the detriment of everybody up until now. Some kind of socialized world society is the only reasonable alternative to the present chaos. Like many of the radical student groups, I favour the weakening of nationalism, but I do not want the abolition of the nation. That would be to remove people still further from the sources of laws and decisions which govern their lives and to work against the principle of self-determination for groups, which I think is almost as important as individual freedom. It seems likely, however, that the meaningful geographical divisions in the future may be regional rather than national. It is certainly improbable that the contemporary boundaries between nations will prove feasible for centuries to come.

As I indicated earlier, I cannot go along with the levelling process which characterizes so much of revolutionary thought. Although it is offered in the guise of liberation for all, its methods and goal smack too much of the Procrustean. One can understand why a programme like that of Mao Tse-tung appears justified as a temporary measure; even so it seems to me to sacrifice too many individuals of the present generation. As a model for a future society, it is hopelessly one-sided in its sentimental glorification of the industrial worker and the peasant. The demands of material productivity have resulted in the sacrifice of all other human needs as surely as in the denounced capitalistic countries. Here, too, the claims of love have been cut short. If the emergency programme should become a permanent structure, China would offer one more example in the dreary list of revolutions which have replaced one form of repression by another. I see no reason to get rid of the Establishment and reform the present system if we are to destroy the individual's freedom to seek the kind of self-fulfilment which he finds to be best for himself and if we are simply to change the shape of the mould into which everyone is fitted. Society as a whole ought to be responsible for guaranteeing concretely the opportunity to each man to live the life he wishes with the absolute minimum of restrictions necessary to protect the rights of others. If we interpret this ideal actively and not passively, it is the very opposite of the Objectivists' doctrine of 'Hands Off' and *laissez-faire*. Possibly it is the same ideal which existing democracies profess to cherish; it is emphatically not the actuality which they promote.[1]

Much has been said recently in denunciation of the Puritan ethic. It is an exaggeration to say that Puritanism continues to be the primary force in dictating Anglo-Saxon cultural attitudes. This is no longer true even in the United States. Furthermore, it is a falsification to interpret this ethic in purely negative terms. Yet there is some truth in the criticism. In particular, what we might more accurately call the Protestant ethic has worked against the natural development of a more humane code of sexual morality and marriage, though no more so than the Catholic ethic or the even more backward teachings of Islam. Several critics have pointed to the influence of the Puritan ideal of self-discipline and distrust of pleasure upon the generally accepted notion that young people in the process of being educated should be asked to work hard and not expect education to be fun; they have noted the irony of such precepts in the midst of a society which constantly praises the joys of leisure and affluence. The Calvinist 'gospel of work', combined with our deep-rooted conviction that

---

[1] It is interesting to note that many of the students in the early protests at Berkeley claimed to be demanding nothing more than the actualization and fulfilment of the guarantees set forth in the Constitution of the United States.

nobody should receive a reward he has not earned, has resulted in a social attitude which may or may not be rational but is certainly devoid of love. This is the real objection to the 'Hippies'. Not only do they declare that they will not work and do not want the material rewards of a steady salary, but they want to claim all the public benefits of those who pay taxes! At either the beginning or the end of human society, I can see that there might be an excuse for a strict equating of contributions and rewards and for the decision to count as expendable persons who, for reasons intelligible only to themselves, will not carry their share of the public burden. In an age of acute scarcity when there is simply not enough of necessities to support everyone, those who eliminate themselves from the struggle are justly the first to suffer. If through total lack of planning we should reach the point where the earth literally could not support the population, there, too, men might find it just to refuse to sustain those who contributed nothing. At present and in the immediate future (granted a significant degree of even voluntary birth control), the world, if its economy were planned from 'the collective will to act humanely' instead of in terms of the special interests of the already established, could and ought to be less grudging in allotting the bare necessities of existence to everyone.

Obviously the first task is to work out a world economy which is capable of preventing sheer starvation and malnutrition. Personally, I do not see how this can be done without both public education and equitable legislation concerning birth control. In any case, I believe it is possible and imperative to create a society in which there may be assurance of more than the right to struggle to keep oneself alive. If we are to give its due to the abstract principle of love, then I firmly believe that everyone ought to be entitled to a certain minimum amount of money, goods, and services without his being required to earn it or show that he deserves it. Naturally I do not advocate that the subsistence thus gratuitously furnished should be at a level and of a quality which most people would find satisfying. It should certainly provide for any person of any age the means to obtain food, shelter, clothes, and medical supplies or treatment. I am convinced that very few persons of normal intelligence and physical health would be satisfied for an extended period of time to live under these meagre conditions of total dependency, particularly not in a society which was making every effort to enable its citizens to develop their individual capacities for creative work and which offered worthwhile incentives for those who were ambitious. We are speaking of the minority – the physically or psychologically weak or wounded. Many contemporary states will grudgingly do something of the sort now for those who are helplessly ill physically or mentally. But in addition to urging that the support be given more thoughtfully, more humanely, and without social stigma for the recipient, I should like to see it greatly extended. Let it be given to the young person who wants to knock about for a year until he finds the way of life to which he can willingly commit himself. Small communities which want to experiment with older forms of living close to the soil should be allowed to do so with the knowledge that the sick child will not be allowed to die because of the parents' poverty and that crop failure would not bring starvation. People who for psychological reasons find themselves unable to cope with life should be helped to find what peace their tormented lives will allow them. This means that there should be a drastic revision in ways of dealing with the neurotic and the psychotic, both in the efforts made to cure them and in the institutions in which the incurable are maintained. Let the drug addict who fails to respond to all efforts to cure him dream away his life without being hounded by the police or feel driven to commit a crime for the sake of the only means he knows for tolerating existence. I am unimpressed by the arguments of persons who claim that kindly treatment of the misfits would result in our being overwhelmed by the numbers of those who would take illicit advantage of the situation. Such cynicism presumes the continuation of all the things which have led so many of this generation to drop out rather than to support a society and a way of life which they have labelled unjust or insane or both. Unless one is totally cynical about the possibilities of human happiness and the worthwhileness of existence, I find it illogical to suppose that very many people will voluntarily choose illusion through drugs or life at the lowest level unless they feel driven to it by forces beyond their control.

The average person may be persuaded to support the proposition that we can afford and are morally obligated to make better provision for the weak, for the abnormal as for the subnormal, perhaps even for the misguided idealists. He will go so far as to favour in a vague sort of way the cause of prison reform and the view that we should make a better effort to prevent crime and to rehabilitate the convict. He will probably draw the line against showing any benevolence toward the criminal. I agree that we ought to make a sharp distinction between people who are incapable or have not learned how to assume their proper share of the public burden and those who deliberately abuse others for their own advantage. I believe that crime would be immeasurably reduced if everyone were guaranteed a livelihood in a state based on a more humane set of principles, and if both the educational system and the possibilities of psychological counselling were developed so as to be able to meet the diverse needs of a great variety of types of human beings. I am not so naïve, so optimistic, or so charitable as to think that, in even the perfectly rational and loving society, there would not be some individuals who will want to commit violence or fraud against others, out of anger or the desire for luxuries and privileges which they are unwilling to work for in accepted ways. I hope it goes without saying that capital punishment, torture, or any punishment which satisfies the vindictive desires of the self-righteous rather than the need to protect potential victims is indefensible and rejected without further consideration. Having long lost my faith in the universal and innate goodness of man, I do not envision a society where there will be absolutely no need for any threat of penalty or restriction of movement to deter those who might otherwise injure others. I cannot imagine a world without traffic laws, for example, and we all realize the chaos which would result if we had no check other than our own discretion with respect to all those acts which would not be harmful on Robinson Crusoe's island but are disastrous in the world as we know it. Even if we are convinced that criminal conduct is always self-defeating and even if our hopes for the future of psychology are unlimited, I assume that the human race will always include a minority of persons who are guilty of seriously asocial and injurious acts, who cannot be persuaded to change, and who must be prevented from harming those with whom they come in contact. Whatever we may call the future substitutes for prisons, they should not be places in which the inmates are deliberately punished and degraded. They ought rather to be the best possible schools and hospitals where the residents would be deprived of some freedom of movement but allowed to lead lives which are not pure suffering and where they are not reduced to the level of objects.

And what of the University in all this and of education generally? Obviously some dramatic changes are called for. Yet it is important to distinguish between error and one-sidedness. Certain current practices are simply wrong and should be abandoned. In many other instances the fault lies not with what we have been doing but with what we have neglected. We have gone too far in the direction of identifying education with the training of scholars, scientists, and technologists; we have tended to equate knowledge with the academic. This does not mean that we should abandon scholarship or discontinue teaching the theoretical sciences and training people for their vocations.

Encouragement and support of the scholar should always be a primary concern in any society and for at least two reasons: First, because the pursuit of knowledge about human achievements and understanding for its own sake remains one of the most intrinsically rewarding of activities and an entirely legitimate means of self-fulfilment for the individual. If we are to encourage any of the arts whose justification is enjoyment, then scholarship maintains its honourable place. In addition, we need the scholar. For the majority of people, a very general knowledge of past and foreign culture is sufficient to give them the sense of perspective which they need if they are not to be imprisoned, to their own detriment, within the provincialities of immediate time and place. Yet the validity and legitimate interpretation of these broad patterns of history and culture depend on the constant accumulation of data and reappraisals which the scholars labour to provide for us. Similarly, we realize that we cannot maintain and increase the well-being of the world's population without trained personnel to keep open communication and transportation systems, to care for our health, to run the industries which we need if we are to be fed, clothed, and provided with the means of protecting ourselves against life-destroying boredom. The theoretical scientist is indispensable, partly for reasons analogous to those which we recognized in the case of the scholar and partly because he must keep the future open for us. Without continuing advance in science and technology, we cannot solve the problems in ecology which the mere fact of our continued existence on this earth has already made acute. It is conceivable that in the years to come, some contact with the resources of outer space may be essential if this cooling and used-up planet is to be able to support life any longer. We need the more extravagant of scientific endeavours as an outlet for our imaginations, our compelling impulse to go forward – in short, to satisfy the pioneer in us who lusts for new frontiers.

In continuing to educate people along these lines and as we support the research of specialists in these areas, we must avoid perpetuating present evils and creating new ones. Although the right to be narrow and one-sided in one's personal life and interests is perhaps as legitimate as any other claim stemming from human psychology, still we must see to it that, before a person gets too deeply involved in the kind of specialization which will render him an authority on Old Icelandic or Ming pottery or the left hindleg of the frog, he will have received a sound education in the contemporary human. We cannot allow the unhindered development of an intellectual genius with the politics of Ezra Pound and the personal *mores* of a Marquis de Sade.

Neither should the experts be permitted to determine the pattern of education for all. The scholar may teach the techniques and accomplishments of scholarship to students who wish to become scholars either as professionals or for their avocations. Unless he is able to use an entirely different approach to his subject as the occasion demands, he and the vast majority of students should be kept far removed from one another for their mutual protection. For the person who does not intend to be a scholar but who wants what deserves to be called a genuinely liberal education, the study of man's history and cultural attainments should indeed be made relevant as the students have been demanding. By 'relevant', I do not mean that every book read, every fact observed must be shown to have a practical bearing on the immediate situation of either the student or contemporary society. Nor do I think it sensible to go to the other extreme and declare that everything is relevant because, as Terence put it, 'Nothing human is alien to me'. Once a young man or woman has reached the level of college, I see no reason why he should be required to study any particular subject unless he is interested in it or needs it as a prerequisite for what he plans to do in the future. Granting the initial motive, he should be able to find that the content of his course of study either is intrinsically interesting or *significantly* increases his understanding of himself and others and his relations to the world at large. There can be no ironclad rule by which we judge relevance, but no self-questioning and honest teacher or student can fail to recognize when it is present or absent. On all occasions the specific needs of individual students should be considered. As I said earlier, there is no reason why all have to meet the same requirements in the same way. Within one small area of subject-matter, a student may legitimately determine how best to work along the lines which are most relevant and meaningful for himself. Nor should the scholar be allowed to prescribe that traditional academic disciplines are the only proper fields of study within a university. Even if we cling to the idea that only the intellectual side of man is the proper concern of an educational institution, I see no reason why the study of contemporary conflict and the possible areas of future development for humanity should be considered non-intellectual. Nor is it logical to assume that the non-verbal is necessarily on the other side of the fence from all that is rational. Emotions and values are as much the raw material of the search for understanding as the study of the circulation of the blood. The development of the highest potentialities of the whole person was considered by Montaigne to be the ideal of the education which he entrusted into the hands of a tutor. It remains more valid as the goal of institutionalized education than most people are willing to admit.

Just as we cannot allow the scholar to define and administer all of the offerings of the University, so we must impose certain strictures and obligations upon the technologists and scientists. Neither must be permitted to forget the end for the means. It is perhaps impossible, without the sacrifice of too many things which we rightly value, to force industry to produce only those articles which satisfy genuine needs instead of those which are artificially cultivated; it is difficult in any case to know just what it is that man needs to live by in additon to bread. Certainly much could be done which has never been attempted. In an economy geared to the needs of a world population, it ought to be possible for industries which now thrive on the ingredients of conspicuous consumption to deal in products of real worth. There should certainly be greater control of the patent, self-defeating false advertising which – along with political propaganda – has gradually undermined our capacity to believe in the truth of any public pronouncement. The development in children of the habit of forming independent judgments in all matters which concern their way of life could ultimately be a greater check to the evils of the business sectors of the Establishment then even increased legal regulations would be. Possibly we might even regain in time the golden era when workmen took pride in their work, business firms in their efficiency, and consumers in the intrinsic worth of their purchases.

The scientist, too, cannot be given an absolutely free rein. Theoretically there should be no limits to free thought and investigation. So long as these remain abstract and speculative, I can see no justification for impeding the search for further understanding. Yet we have always recognized practical limits as in, for example, prohibitions against the vivisection of living people or medical experimentation without the full and knowing consent of the subject. We have reached a point now when other injurious consequences must be considered – for example, research involving radioactivity. As with the scholar, activities which are innocent or positive in themselves may become potentially harmful to mankind if there is a conflict between the interests of a few and the needs of many. The moon flight has become an almost universal symbol here. In many ways it seems to me that the issue has been falsely represented. The funds expended on the first moon landing would almost certainly not have been diverted to the kind of war on poverty which the anti-space demonstrators were demanding. Furthermore, there would be a relative abundance of money available for both domestic needs and space projects if it were not for the collective madness which has chosen to constitute military spending as the ultimate indispensable. Nevertheless, there is, on principle, an inborn conflict between the material needs of present individuals and the demands of scientific investigation for the sake of keeping the way clear for further development of our understanding of the universe. We must find a reasonable compromise between the two demands. It is ridiculous to claim that humanity as a whole does not profit from the great scientific breakthroughs, whether it is in the immediate excitement of sharing in new discoveries or in the later practical consequences. But the speed, rate, and direction of scientific research should not be decided without due calculation of the cost in terms other than monetary. At first thought it seems ironic that at a time when the extraordinarily complex activities of man have required that the work of experts be supplemented by the precision of the computer and the sensitivity of radar, we should be presented with the earnest plea that what we need is 'a generation of generalists'. Paradoxical as this situation is, we must recognize the validity of each point of view. Unless we are to regress or to destroy ourselves, we cannot do without the specialists able to devise and use these machines which have capabilities in many ways beyond the human; we need a generation of educated citizens who can push us toward a better understanding of the needs of the human beings whom science ought to serve.

Student protesters have been forceful champions of the claim that society owes more to its non-intellectuals, not merely to the underprivileged minorities but to the vast majority of the population – the workers. At first thought this matter may appear to be wholly a political issue with no direct bearing on the problems of education; in actuality there is a most important connection. In the first place, I feel strongly that public education should contribute far more than it does toward meeting the needs of those whose interests and abilities are non-intellectual or at least non-verbal. Ivan Illich has stated this very forcefully apropos of Puerto Rico:

> I believe that a youth of thirteen who has received only four years of formal schooling has the right to further advantages greater than those given to a child of the same age who has benefited from eight years of schooling. The more deprived the citizen is, the more he needs to have this right guaranteed to him.[1]

Illich is so disillusioned with the discrepancy between the traditional offerings of schools and the actual needs of children, and he is so moved by the economic injustice of a society where the initially disadvantaged cannot profit from so-called free public education that he has taken the drastic step of proposing that compulsory attendance at school be abolished and an amount of money equal to the *per capita* cost of education be given to parents to use in training children

[1] Ivan Illich, op. cit., p. 681.

as they wish. Presumably they might be able to support the child during a period of apprenticeship while he learned a trade or something of that sort. In my opinion, this proposal would serve only to widen still further the gap between the working class and the intellectual elite. Yet there are two aspects of it which merit our attention.

By implication Illich suggests that, properly speaking, the State's obligation to educate its youth ought to be interpreted as meaning that the State must see to it that each one of its young people is in a position to earn an adequate living when he reaches adulthood. This is not the same as saying that the schools are to teach those rudimentary skills which are the foundation for further study and that those who lack verbal ability should go out and find a job for themselves. For boys and girls who definitely will not profit from academic study, there should be provided not only training for specific vocations but teaching in all those things which will aid them in managing their everyday affairs and in deriving pleasure from leisure-time activities. Another point, which Illich does not bring up but which seems to me equally important, is this: A democracy confronts a situation precisely the opposite of what exists in Maoist China. There – somewhat artificially, to be sure – we find a glorification of the dignity of workers and the granting of privileges to them at the expense of the intellectuals and professionals. In a society based on the principle that incentives and rewards must be provided for out of the ordinary achievement, it is inevitable that a person who has spent years of extra study so as to develop abilities beyond those of the average individual will receive something tangible in return – in money, in power, in special privilege or all three. This is as it should be, and it is hopelessly foolish to expect that there will ever be a strong and healthy society where special reward for special effort is denied. Unfortunately people have always tended to view the possession of these rewards as the outward signs of intrinsic personal value, thus adding the extra emoluments of social prestige and recognized superiority. Perhaps this is a basic inequality in the natural scheme of things which cannot be wiped out completely any more than we can dispel the sadness in the heart of a girl deformed from birth when she looks at a beautiful classmate. There are some things which we could do. From the earliest years of schooling, we can instil in the child the notion that there are many types of successful lives, manifold values, and that his task is to find the style of life which best satisfies him. We can concretely support our faith in this philosophy by fostering within the school system an infinite variety of studies combining in varied proportions academic and non-academic, verbal and non-verbal activities. By stressing the ideals of service and self-fulfilment rather than social approval and material success, we may gradually rub out the scars of centuries of elitism. One thing, of course, is indispensable. It will be of little avail to talk about the dignity of labour and the importance of service if the economic status of workers allows only the lowest level of substance. The minimum wage for every employed person must be adequate to support a life of dignity. Granting this much, we might even go so far as to say that the least pleasant tasks of unskilled labour should be given extra reward by way of compensation. A well-planned economy could support a much higher average level for all and still provide special rewards for the gifted and ambitious.

I do not mean to say, of course, that the educational institutions can accomplish such changes all by themselves. There would have to be corresponding changes in the rest of the social structure. Unions, for example, would have to co-operate in any effective attempt to combine education with apprenticeships. Industrial managements would have to work out, along with school and university administrators, criteria for recognizing adequate preparation for specific positions rather than regarding a high school certificate or college diploma as the union card which it is now. Someone may argue that no matter what we may attempt to teach our children, and regardless of whatever changes we may institute in an effort to supply for each student the schooling which will help him to find and prepare for the life which is best for him, parents will now and forever insist on the usual external trappings of status and prestige. To this I can only respond that, if we cannot change public opinion through education, then I know of no better method. We have to start somewhere, and the most likely as well as the most practical point is there where we stand to influence the rising generation of future parents and teachers.

The other half of Illich's suggestion is more revolutionary – that funds for education should not be given to school officials but directly to the parents. I cannot go along with his proposal in exactly this form, for I believe that the child needs protection against the weaknesses and limitations of his father and mother as well as against the centralized authority of the State. Nevertheless there is possibly some merit in the idea that there might be a better means of distributing and using public funds than to entrust them to the school board of a city or county for maintaining a series of standard institutions. George Dennison presents a persuasive argument to this effect in *The Lives of Children*. The book relates the experiences of two years' work in a private, experimental school established in lower East side, New York. There were only twenty-three pupils, all of them children who in one way or another were in trouble in the public schools; they came from families who were on welfare or too poor to afford tuition. The venture was spectacularly successful, but the school was closed for lack of funds when

the private grant which had been provided for the experiment
was exhausted. Dennison points out that the annual cost for
each child was just about the same as the amount of money
which New York spends yearly for every pupil in the public
system. Without extra taxation it would be possible to
support small schools designed either to help children with
special needs or to experiment with new approaches to
education which might ultimately modify the methods of
the average school. Dennison and his associates were concerned with what we significantly call 'problem children'.
The results showed that in almost every case the child's
problems were capable of solution; at least the boy or girl
showed marked improvement. Part of the explanation may
lie in the fact that the enrolment was small and that the
teachers, in addition to being especially well trained, really
cared about each of the children as an individual and were
enthusiastic about what was being accomplished. This was
not all. In speaking of what distinguished the First Street
School, Dennison says,

Where the public school conceives of itself merely as a place of
instruction, and puts severe restraints on the relationships between
persons, we conceived of ourselves as an environment for growth,
and accepted the relationships between the children and ourselves as
being the very heart of the school.[1]

His philosophy of elementary education is summed up in a
single sentence. 'The business of a school is not, or should
not be, mere instruction but the life of the child.' Consequently he and the other teachers insisted that they were not

[1] George Dennison, *The Lives of Children*, New York, Random House,
1970. I was unable to obtain the book itself before completing the
manuscript for this work. I am indebted for the account of school
and quotations from the book to a detailed review in *The New Yorker*
by Nat Hentoff, 7 March 1970. pp. 116-20.

teaching subjects but children. In a programme both ungraded and unstructured, the teachers learned to understand the child and to help him understand himself until he learned to strike out on his own path. At the end of the two years, some of the pupils who had been unable to read, for example, now were able to read at a level considered appropriate for several years beyond their actual age. There were no formal classes in reading, writing, arithmetic, and the other rudimentary subjects, but the children learned these as well as non-verbal skills in activities which they engaged in voluntarily both as individuals and as groups.

There have been a number of other schools, some of them developed within the public school system, which have sought to combine the insights of psychotherapy and in-dividual imagination and with encouraging results. Almost always these projects have been designed to give a headstart to the underprivileged or to help the misfits. It seems to me that the approach is to be recommended for all of the early years of education. Some concrete subject-matter must be learned sooner or later, and it is perfectly true that one must have something definite to talk about or to work at in order to develop critical thinking and creativity of any kind. I do not think that this fact necessitates or justifies our assumption that graded progress through the various disciplines is properly the cornerstone of the educational process. During at least the elementary years, reading, arithmetic, and the like should be considered as tools and material – like paper, crayons, and picture books. The essential task is to enable the child to discover himself, to explore some of the possible ways of relating himself to the world, and to learn satisfying ways of living and working with others. The ideal teacher would not only be trained to recognize and deal with psychological conflicts but prepared to help the child understand his own emotions and to realize his responsibilities toward others.

Within the school situation, the teacher should try to teach what we may unabashedly call the art of living; like any instructor in the arts, he or she must have practised the art personally and be able to communicate the fruits of experience while remembering that the aim is to enable the child to develop his own talents and not merely to imitate.

I think that the unstructured programme ought to be extended throughout the whole of the educational system. Obviously there must be certain points at which a person must show that he is ready to leave an institution at a lower level and to advance to a higher one. I see no reason why his progress up to that point has to be so strictly regimented and divided into fixed grades and classes as it is now. At the higher levels when the mastery of certain subject-matter is essential, there is obviously need for some means of assuring that the minimum of factual material has been learned. I do not propose, for example, that a student going through medical school should be allowed to study only those diseases and parts of the anatomy which happen to interest him and then announce that he is ready to move on when he feels like it. But the memorization of facts and the acquiring of technical skills, while they may be absolute requirements for anyone wishing to undertake certain professions, should not be considered as the sole end and criterion of an education at any stage and especially not in the final years of graduate school. There, too, the proper goal of education is the individual's self-discovery and free creation of himself as a human being who has chosen to be a physician or chemist, lawyer or sociologist, who must practise his profession in a world where there are others with needs both like and unlike his own. We can be justly proud of what our education has accomplished in the way of solving scientific problems and answering the questions of scholarship. I am unwilling to admit that we must forever stand baffled before the philosophical and psychological demands of those who ask that they be taught those things which will help them to make life worth living.

The area of eschatology which offers the most extravagant promises and the worst of nightmare threats is the field of biological research. Here we confront directly the prospect of the directed evolution of the human species as well as the potential fulfilment of those dreams which once seemed to belong only with the unreal fantasies of science fiction – death indefinitely postponed, living on borrowed or artificial vital organs, pre-natal determination of the physiology and personality of individuals, mind-tampering drugs, perhaps even the achievement of new forms of consciousness and extrasensory perception. Here more than anywhere else we need the constant interaction of love and reason as we move through the twilight regions of research which no longer aims at understanding life but at modifying, reconstituting, and creating it.

A striking example of the danger which lies in the blind acceptance of all scientific achievement as intrinsically good is found in *The Biological Time Bomb* by Gordon Rattray Taylor. Although Taylor shows more of the journalist's zeal for the sensational than is pleasing to most scientists, he is remarkably persuasive in pointing out the probability that, if we do not adequately plan for our future, it will destroy us. Taylor takes it for granted that, with the need for population control, genetic regulation will be adapted. With remarkable lack of any sign of emotion, he writes the following paragraph:

It is curious to reflect that the great spiritual philosopher, J. E. Renan, in his *Dialogues*, saw in eugenics a transcendent possibility. 'A far-reaching application of physiology and of the principle of selection', he said as long ago as 1871, 'might lead to the creation of a superior race, whose right to govern would reside not only in its science, but in the very superiority of its blood, its brain, its nervous system'. There would be joy in submitting to them, he said, for they would be 'incarnations of the divine'. Perhaps, after all, it will be the French who first introduce positive eugenics.[1]

The thought that Renan's earthly deities might be the logical outcome of 'positive eugenics' is horrifying to me. Yet it is perfectly consistent with the notion that scientific research must be allowed to develop freely so long as its consequences are not demonstrably injurious to anyone. Following as a natural corollary is the assumption that it is better to benefit a few individuals than to reject something good simply because not everyone can share in it. Put abstractly and theoretically, both of these principles seem sound enough. Certainly it would be mean spirited in the extreme to insist that two heart patients be allowed to die rather than to give a transplant to only one of them. If we allow this kind of reasoning to give free rein to the application of biological technology, unchecked by other considerations, we might very well end up with a physiologically determined caste system to which I, for one, am firmly opposed. If the adoption of 'positive eugenics' is to be accompanied by legislation to prohibit all but a select few from reproducing themselves, then it seems to me that it is a negatively repressive programme, no matter how hard we try to disguise its true nature. Genetic coding may well have certain possibilities of good for all mankind, but I would not support a programme with the intended consequence of preparing for the eventual dominance of a single human type, deemed desirable by only part of the world's population.

Many persons arguing on what they at least believe to be purely rational grounds, would hold that in the long run it would be better for all if we did everything possible to develop

[1] Gordon Rattray Taylor, *The Biological Time Bomb*, New York, World Publishing Co., 1968, p. 180; London, Thames & Hudson, 1968.

a superior species of human in the distant future without worrying about intervening generations. Some would even go so far as to accept Renan's suggestion, feeling that so long as the subspecies of the new humanity was content with the role of obedience and devotion to the super-beings, the creation of the latter would be completely justified. To my mind these are at best the claims of objective reason untouched by love, and I reject them. At the same time I should not want to have my objection interpreted as meaning that I should advocate that all research in genetic coding, for example, should be prohibited or that we should not attempt to devise ways in which we might develop some of the constructive possibilities in eugenics without either repressive legislation or the deepening of class cleavages. What is most important, of course, is to realize that in matters like these no individual nor small group should be allowed to decide for the whole of mankind, regardless of its members' confidence in their own qualifications and objectivity. Perhaps the first and primary task before us is to work out as quickly as possible some procedure for dealing with those questions which have implication for the future but call for decisions which must be made here and now. Two things are necessary. One is an abundance of discussion of all these matters, both by various experts and by the general public. It has been encouraging to read reports of symposia devoted to the problems of the future or, with more appeal to dramatic imagination, to discussion of mankind's situation in the year 2000.[1] The second is to set up the actual machinery for decision making, and here society has understandably moved very slowly. The Law has been forced to take cognizance of some of the

[1] G. R. Taylor points out that *Daedalus* published 'a number of studies of the year 2000' in its issue for Summer 1967 and that 'the first major international meeting devoted to this subject was held in September 1967 under the title *Mankind 2000*'. Ibid., p. 228.

dilemmas stemming from the practice of making organ transplants, but we have not got much beyond this point. I do not propose that members of the University or any group of scientists or intellectuals should simply be entrusted with the power to determine the future for humanity. At the same time I believe that the University, more than any other single institution, will be and ought to be active both in taking the lead in discussion of such issues and in arriving at significant decisions.

Taylor offers the possibility that a 'strong Social Sciences Council' might serve as an advisory council for the government; he urges also that 'Universities should be establishing chairs of social prediction'.[1] These are both good suggestions, but they do not take us very far. Within the University there should be inter-disciplinary courses designed specifically to study the implications of new discoveries in scientific research, to discuss in anticipation both the positive and negative possibilities in man's 'future-perfect'. Our belated recognition of the urgency of problems in ecology has already led some universities to introduce a programme of studies in 'the environment' where the emphasis is as much on the probable developments of the next hundred years as on the immediate difficulties of pollution and overpopulation which have already become manifest. We need more of such organized plans for specific studies, but that is not enough. The temper of the University as a whole should be more oriented toward the future than it has ever been since its establishment in the Middle Ages. Naturally I do not mean that we can abandon all study of the past, still less of the present. But we ought also to encourage students, especially at the graduate level, to use their creative imaginations in looking forward. A doctoral dissertation which proposed a new solution for a current sociological problem would be at least as valuable

[1] Taylor, G.R., op. cit., pp. 226-7.

for both its author and the taxpayers as an objective analysis of social patterns in a given segment of present or past society. One can imagine students in psychology and philosophy and even literature occasionally writing a thesis aimed at helping rather than recording man's search for meaning. In the pure sciences, professors and students alike should be forced to discuss the relevance of their work to ethical and social questions. It would be helpful to have a university committee concerned with recognizing the emergence of the new problems and possibilities from scientific breakthroughs; where appropriate it might make recommendations to the government for legislation or social action.

I do not pretend to know precisely what machinery ought to be set up for making the new 'eschatological' decisions. Whatever plan we initiated would undoubtedly have to be subject to later modifications. Of one thing I feel sure. Any council entrusted with the task of determining the direction of scientific developments should include the scientists themselves but not be composed exclusively of those who carry on the research. We need the special knowledge of the expert, but it must be accompanied by the opinion of the layman who will have to live with the consequences. The chief function of such a council might be to serve as a watchdog, to guarantee that the public is kept informed so that we are neither unknowingly pushed in a direction which we would not have chosen nor confronted with life and death decisions for which there has been no preparation.

From the vantage point of our present understanding of the universe, it seems to me most appropriate to think of man as sustaining a partnership with nature. To say that he is a partner is not to make him simply a part. I do not believe that our proper destiny lies in accepting ourselves simply as the conditioned products of natural forces nor in seeking to find a neo-primitive mode of existence which would provide for us instinctual nourishment and certainty comparable to what is enjoyed by the other animals. It is our ability to separate ourselves from nature in our thought which gives us control over our future. As a partner, however, we can no more abuse or ignore nature than a captain can show disrespect for his ship or a sculptor for his materials. One absolute limit for individual freedom in the future must be respect for the environment on which the existence of all of us depends.

If we give free rein to our imagination, then it is an all but irresistible temptation to postulate the possibility that at some distant date we might pull away still another of the veils surrounding the inner essence of things and reveal an entirely different view of reality and our relations with it. The claim of religion, of course, is that, through revelation or faith or mystic experience, the veil has already been momentarily lifted and that the attendant vision justifies our rejection of the scientific view that the physical universe is impersonal and without purpose. In speaking of the clearing of new vistas in the future, I am not thinking of the possibility that we might ultimately validate for all the moments of cosmic insight now claimed by a few. I refer rather to the theoretical possibility that we might uncover any one of a number of situations which would totally transform human existence as we have known it, possibly to the extent that we might genuinely question whether it should any longer be called human. I can best illustrate my point by referring to two illustrations offered by Voltaire in his philosophical novella, *Candide*, and William James in an essay called 'Is Life Worth Living?'

When Candide complained to the Dervish about the evil and suffering in the world, the Dervish responded with a question: 'When his Highness sends a ship to Egypt, does he worry about the comfort or discomfort of the rats in the ship?' Candide concluded that, since the Universe offered no sense or purpose nor even a sympathetic environment for humans, he had best leave off searching and questioning and derive a subdued contentment from cultivating his own garden. Voltaire felt that the existence of his Highness' purpose was irrelevant since it was in no way commensurate with that of the rats. James illustrates this same sense of a meaning that is beyond reach by the example of a dog which is subjected to painful tests in the laboratory for the sake of furthering human knowledge. But James derives a totally different moral. Sentimentally he argues that, if somehow the animal could know that its sufferings were furthering a higher purpose, it would be comforted. My first reaction is to be offended by this analogy. Even if the dog could be told that he was helping to achieve goals not his own, how could this information mean any more to him than a comparable message to the rats in his Highness' ship? True, the dog is mistreated deliberately rather than incidentally, but being used as a tormented living instrument for another's advantage is hardly better than being ignored. James' 'if' appears illegitimate in any case since the dog does not and cannot know. This is exactly the point. In James' comparison, man is not like the real dog but resembles a hypothetical dog which could gradually learn the now obscure motives of the technicians. Once he understood them, he might indeed be comforted and willingly participate in the experiments. For then (James himself scarcely goes this far) the dog would no longer be the uncomprehending creature he is now. Goals his mind could grasp would be, if he chose, *his* goals. Ought he so to choose? Or having advanced to this stage, would he do better to use his newly won skills to search for his own meaning and way of life in a universe over which his consciousness exerted new control and power? Should he worship his god-man as master or revolt against him?

Having only a human point of view, I cannot say how the dog should decide.

Without pushing the details of the analogy too closely, I suggest that man may someday find himself in a position roughly equivalent to that of James' evolved dog. It could happen in any number of different ways. We could encounter another race of conscious beings more advanced than our own. We might reveal in the structure of the universe the existence of a purpose which was not a 'human' purpose – one which at present we could neither understand nor imagine. Or we may discover ways whereby our descendants might evolve into another kind of being, too different from us to be considered any longer as of the same species with us. This last possibility seems to me to constitute the ultimate limit of self-transcendence. If it should come about as the result of free and united human will to thrust forward, then perhaps it is the one ideal to which man might legitimately sacrifice himself. Even this would not justify the sacrifice of some men by others. In the final impulse toward self-transcendence as in each intervening step between now and then, all hope of justifying our actions requires that we listen to the demands of love as well as seeking to satisfy the thirst of reason. Love reminds us that reverence for the need of every individual is the sole support of human solidarity.

I have said that the University as the new Church should concern itself with eschatology and with the problem of values. I think that its involvement with the community should be much closer than it is at present and that it ought to be willing to accept the responsibilities of guardian of the public conscience. At the same time the University should guard against repeating some of the mistakes of the medieval Church. It must resist the temptation to think that men may be saved only through its offices. It cannot afford to create a new gap between laity and overprivileged clergy. Under no circumstances may it rely on past revelation or lay claim to an unchallenged spiritual authority. It is both the leader and the servant of humanity but it has not been entrusted with the mission of serving as the representative of a god. In some ways, perhaps, we could say that the University is providing – or ought to provide – those things which traditionally have been said to derive from God. If our philosophy of education adequately fulfilled the ideal of reason combined with love, then those who came to the University campus ought to find ways of self-fulfilment and a meaning for their personal lives, a sense of their place in the unfolding of a historical plan and their participation in the community. They would be offered the opportunity of sharing in that kind of immortality which comes from knowing that what one has contributed to change the world lives on after personal death. If we are to consider that man's original sin is wilful ignorance and blindness to responsibilities, then the University can hope to supply the grace necessary for salvation. The underlying faith of the University in its own mission should rest simply on the conviction that all men and women are worth saving.

BIBLIOGRAPHY

It is obviously impossible to list all of the important books and articles which have been written about the crisis in contemporary education. The following have either been quoted in this book or have been particularly relevant – though not always sympathetic – to the point of view which I have presented.

BARTH, JOHN, *Giles Goat-Boy or, The Revised New Syllabus*, Garden City, N.Y., Doubleday, 1966; London, Secker & Warburg, 1967.

China Pictorial. Relevant articles of interest are included in the following issues: Nos. 10 and 12 in 1968 and Nos. 1 and 3 in 1969. Published in Peking.

China Reconstructs. In addition to articles listed by author, there are anonymous articles of particular interest in the issues for November and December 1968. Published in Peking.

COHN-BENDIT, DANIEL, Interview published in *Magazine Littéraire*, May 1968.

Daedalus. Two special issues have been devoted to the study of the problems of the University: Fall 1969 and Winter 1970. *Daedalus* is the Journal of the American Academy of Arts and Sciences.

DENNISON, GEORGE, *The Lives of Children*, New York, Random House, 1970.

ELVIN, H. L., *Education and Contemporary Society*, London, C. A. Watts, The New Thinker's Library, 1965.

FLETCHER, JOSEPH, *Situation Ethics: The New Morality*, Philadelphia, Westminster Press, 1966; London, S.C.M. Press, 1966.

FYODOROV, K., 'Western Youth and Ideological Struggle', *International Affairs*, published in Moscow, September 1968, pp. 76–82.

GALKIN, A., ' "Neocapitalism" and the Facts', *International Affairs*, published in Moscow, November 1968, pp. 31–6.

HAYDEN, TOM, 'Two, Three, Many Columbias', *Ramparts*, 15 June 1968, p. 40.

ILLICH, IVAN, 'L'École, cette Vache Sacrée', *Les Temps modernes*, November 1969, pp. 673–83.

JENCKS, CHRISTOPHER, and RIESMAN, DAVID, *The Academic Revolution*, Garden City, N.Y., Doubleday, 1968.

KEATS, JOHN, *The Sheepskin Psychosis*, New York, Dell, Laurel Edition, 1967.

LAING, R. D., *The Politics of Experience*, New York, Pantheon Books, 1967; Harmondsworth, Penguin Books, 1967.

LANGFORD, THOMAS A., 'Campus Turmoil: A Religious Dimension', *The Christian Century*, 8 February 1967, pp. 172–4.

LEACH, EDMUND R., 'We Scientists Have the Right to Play God', *Saturday Evening Post*, 16 November 1968, pp. 16 and 20.

LEJEUNE, ANTHONY, 'Violence: Tool of Demagogues', *Daily Telegraph*, the 'Opinion' page, 28 June 1968.

MARCUSE, HERBERT, *One Dimensional Man*, London, Routledge & Kegan Paul, 1964.

MARCUSE, HERBERT, MOORE, BARRINGTON, JR., and WOLFF, ROBERT PAUL, *A Critique of Pure Tolerance*, Boston, Beacon Press, 1965.

MARIN, YURI V., 'Party Press Attacks "Leftist Extremism",' *Analysis of Current Developments in the Soviet Union*, published by Institute for the Study of the USSR, in Munich, No. 552, 10 June 1969.

McLUHAN, MARSHALL and FIORE, QUENTIN, *The Medium Is the Massage: An Inventory of Effects*, New York, Bantam, 1967; London, Penguin Press, 1967.

MEAD, MARGARET, *Culture and Commitment: A Study of the Generation Gap*, Garden City, N.Y., The Natural History Press, 1970.

MORRIS, DESMOND, *The Naked Ape*, New York, Dell, 1969; London, Cape, 1967.

POSTMAN, NEIL, and WEINGARTNER, CHARLES, *Teaching as a Subversive Activity*, New York, Delacorte Press, 1969.

Peking Review. In addition to articles listed by author, there are anonymous articles of particular interest in the following issues published in 1968: 17 May, 31 May, 8 November, 13 December. Published in Peking.

PICKERING, SIR GEORGE, *The Challenge to Education*, London, C. A. Watts, The New Thinker's Library, 1967.

'The Playboy Panel: Student Revolt', *Playboy*, September 1969, pp. 89–116 and 233–49.

POIRIER, RICHARD, 'The War Against the Young', *The Atlantic*, October 1968, pp. 55–64.

SARTRE, JEAN-PAUL, *Critique de la raison dialectique*, Paris, Gallimard, 1960. This includes the essay 'Question de méthode'. The latter has been published under the title *Search for a Method*, translated by Hazel E. Barnes, New York, Knopf, 1963. The same translation was published in England under the title *The Problem of Method*, London, Methuen.

TAYLOR, GORDON RATTRAY, *The Biological Time Bomb*, New York, World Publishing Co., 1968; London, Thames & Hudson, 1968.

TAYLOR, HAROLD, *Students without Teachers: The Crisis in the University*, London and New York, McGraw-Hill, 1969.

TENG WEN-YU, 'Honestly Receive Re-Education by the Working Class', *Peking Review*, 1 August 1968, pp. 15–17.

TOYNBEE, PHILIP, 'Intolerable', *Observer Review*, 23 June 1968, pp. 21–2.

VORONITSYN, SERGEI S., 'No Feather-Bedding in Soviet Higher Education', *Analysis of Current Developments in the Soviet Union*, published by Institute for the Study of the USSR, in Munich, No. 540, 18 March 1969.

WALLERSTEIN, IMMANUEL, *University in Turmoil: The Politics of Change*, New York, Atheneum, 1969.

WIDGERY, DAVID, 'Universities: Home of Revolution', *Daily Telegraph*, the 'Opinion' page, 28 June, 1968.

WILLIAMS, GEORGE, *Some of My Best Friends Are Professors: A Critical Commentary on Higher Education*, London and New York, Abelard-Schuman, 1958.

Wilson, Bryan R., *Religion in Secular Society: A Sociological Comment*, London, C. A. Watts, The New Thinker's Library, 1966.

Yao Wen-yuan, 'The Working Class Must Exercise Leadership in Everything', *China Reconstructs*, November 1968, pp. 4–8.

INDEX